Reflections of
Osiris

Reflections of Osiris
Lives from Ancient Egypt

JOHN RAY

2002

OXFORD
UNIVERSITY PRESS

Oxford   New York
Auckland   Bangkok   Buenos Aires
Cape Town   Chennai   Dar es Salaam   Delhi   Hong Kong   Istanbul
Karachi   Kolkata   Kuala Lumpur   Madrid   Melbourne   Mexico City   Mumbai
Nairobi   São Paulo   Shanghai   Singapore   Taipei   Tokyo   Toronto

and an associated company in

Berlin

Published by Oxford University Press, Inc.
198 Madison Avenue, New York, New York 10016

Oxford is a registered trademark of Oxford University Press

Library of Congress Cataloging-in-Publication Data
Ray, John.
Reflections of Osiris : lives from ancient Egypt / John Ray.
p. cm.
Includes bibliographic references and index.
ISBN 0-19-515871-7 (alk. paper)
1. Egypt--Civilization--To 332 B.C. 2. Egypt--Civilization--
332 B.C.-30 B.C. 3. Osiris (Egyptian deity) I. Title.

DT61 R25 2002
932'.01--dc
2002070027

1 3 5 7 9 10 8 6 4 2
Printed in the United States of America
on acid-free paper

For Dorothy Thompson, John Thompson, and
Frank Walbank, who know why people study ancient Egypt,
and need not trouble to read this book

Contents

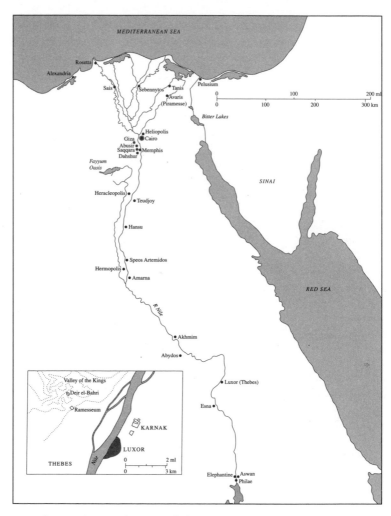

Map of Egypt, showing the principal places mentioned in the text. The inset shows the area of Thebes, modern Luxor.

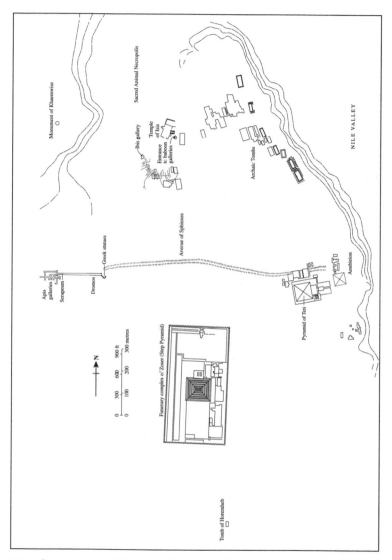

Map of Saqqara, part of the necropolis of Memphis, with the principal places mentioned in the text.

A Note on Chronology and Names

THE HISTORY of ancient Egypt is long, and authorities do not agree on precise dates. After 500 BC the chronology is as good as fixed. Before this, there is a margin of error of some fifty years for dates going back to 1500 BC, and a likelihood of up to a hundred years for periods earlier than this. The conventional division into dynasties is convenient, if oversimplified, and it is followed here. Similarly for convenience, I have followed the dating given in *The Oxford Illustrated History of Ancient Egypt* (ed. Ian Shaw, Oxford, 2000). However, the dates given here for the Eighteenth Dynasty may need to be raised, partly for reasons connected with astronomy, partly because of the uncertainty affecting the Amarna period and the reign of Horemheb.

Archaic Period (Dynasties 'O', I and II)   c. 3200–2686 BC
This period saw the emergence of the Egyptian centralised state, and the foundations of Pharaonic government. Egyptian art took on many of its characteristic forms during the first two dynasties. The royal burials were mostly at the site of Abydos in Upper Egypt.

Old Kingdom (Dynasties III–VI) c. 2686–2160

The Old Kingdom is often referred to as the Pyramid Age. During this period Egyptian art reached a peak of its development, and monumental architecture proliferated. The first literary and religious texts made their appearance. Memphis was the seat of government, and kings and courtiers were buried in the necropolis of Giza and Saqqara.

Imhotep
c. 2650

First Intermediate Period (Dynasties VII–X) c. 2160–2055

The collapse of central authority led to fragmentation, civil war and political disruption. This was brought to an end by the rise of a princely family at Thebes (modern Luxor), which succeeded in reuniting the country.

Middle Kingdom (Dynasties XI–XIII) c. 2055–1650

The Middle Kingdom saw a flowering of literature and the arts, and was regarded by the Egyptians of later periods as a classic age. The Fayyum oasis was developed for agriculture, and the seat of government moved to a new capital, Itj-tawy, which lay south of Memphis on the way to the entrance to the Fayyum. The area of Lower Nubia, between the First and Second Cataracts, became an Egyptian colony.

Heqanakhte
c. 1950

Twelfth Dynasty c. 1985–1773

Second Intermediate Period (Dynasties XIV–XVII) c. 1650–1550

Central government collapsed again, and settlers from the Near

East took advantage of this weakness to occupy much of Lower Egypt, ruling from the city of Avaris in the Delta. These are known to later tradition as the Hyksos. A family from Thebes, conventionally listed as Dynasty XVII, succeeded in driving out the invaders and reunifying the country.

New Kingdom (Dynasties XVIII–XX)   c. 1550–1069
The expulsion of the Hyksos led to a new militarism, and the establishment of something resembling an empire in Syria and Palestine. Upper Nubia (the area along the Nile in the northern Sudan) was occupied and Egyptianised. Wealth and exotic splendour increased, and influenced both literature and the visual arts. Royal burials moved from the north of the country to the Valley of the Kings on the west bank at Thebes.

Eighteenth Dynasty   c. 1550–1295

Hatshepsut   reigned c. 1473–1458

Horemheb   reigned c. 1323–1295 (?)

Nineteenth Dynasty   c. 1295–1186

Ramesses II   reigned c. 1279–1213

Khaemwise   lived c. 1285–1225

Late New Kingdom or Third Intermediate Period (Dynasties XXI–XXV)   c. 1089–664

The New Kingdom declined slowly, and the collapse of the Twentieth Dynasty led to a political division of the country, with a series of dynasties ruling Lower Egypt from the newly founded city of Tanis, while an overlapping series ruled Upper Egypt from Thebes. The interlude was one of straightened circumstances, but not of the anarchy which characterised the first two Intermediate Periods.

Late Period (Dynasties XXVI–XXX)   664–323

Reunification of the country was once more achieved, but at the price of employing foreign mercenaries and expertise. Immigration from the eastern Mediterranean gained pace, and this needed to be counterbalanced by emphasising the traditional aspects of Egyptian culture. This is particularly evident in the visual art of the period. The Persian conquest of the country (525–404 BC) did nothing to diminish these tendencies. This was followed by a short period of renewed independence in the fourth century BC.

Twenty-Sixth Dynasty   664–525

Persian Conquest   525

Petiese   lived c. 583–511

Departure of Persians   404

Nectanebo II   reigned 359/8–343/2

Alexander the Great arrives in Egypt 332

Ptolemaic Period 323–30 BC
The conquest by Alexander led to the establishment of Greek rule
and the formation of the cosmopolitan city of Alexandria. Government of the country used the Greek language alongside the Egyptian, which was written both in hieroglyphs and in the vernacular
demotic script. A synthesis of Greek and Egyptian culture developed, both in literature and in the visual arts.

Hor of Sebennytos lived c. 200–150

Death of Cleopatra and Roman annexation of Egypt 30 BC

Roman Period 30 BC–c. AD 395
Egypt became a province of the Roman empire after the suicide of
Antony and Cleopatra. However, unlike other provinces, it remained under the direct control of the emperor, who was represented by a Prefect. Temple building and other traditional
activities continued down to the fourth century AD. Conversely,
the number of documents written in the Egyptian language begins
to decline.

Coptic or **Byzantine Period** c. AD 395–640
During this period Egypt was nominally ruled from Byzantium
(also known as Constantinople). The Egyptian language was
adapted to the Greek alphabet, and used for Christian purposes,
in which phase it is known as Coptic. Greek continued to be used
as the medium of government and much intellectual life.

Arab Conquest of Egypt AD 640
After the Arab conquest Islam, together with the Arabic language,

made increasing progress. The Coptic language gradually became extinct, probably in the early modern period, although it is still used liturgically. Some 5 per cent of the modern population are Coptic Christian; most of the rest are Sunni Muslims.

I have tried to give proper names in the forms that are familiar from accessible textbooks, but with some compromises, and without any of the diacritical marks favoured by Egyptologists. It is not possible to be consistent in this, which is in the nature of things Egyptological.

Introduction

THIS IS a book about ancient Egypt, intended for those who know a little about an intriguing civilisation and would like to know more. It is also written for those who are curious to find out why people spend their time studying a world that has long passed from history, and a language which has not been heard for centuries. Part of the fascination felt by those who know the subject comes from the tension between those aspects of Egyptology which seem familiar to us, and those which are alien. To frame this contrast within the time and space of individual lives is one way of bringing it home.

The framework I have adopted is a series of semi-biographical chapters, which are intended to throw light on aspects of the society in which these characters lived. As far as the sources permit, I have tried to enter into the thoughts of these characters, and to use this technique to illustrate the civilisation which produced them. Strictly speaking, this will never be possible. Too little is known about any of these persons for us to be certain that we have got the picture right. The characters of the Serapeum, who appear in the final chapter, are something of an exception, because their documents survive in quantity and allow us to see into their thoughts, in a way that is rare in any period. But even here, there is much that the sources take for granted, about which a twenty-first-century student has to guess. The truth is that we cannot write a biography, in the modern sense, of any character in the ancient world, not even Alexander the Great; we have to wait until Julian the Apostate or St Augustine for that. But in a sense this is a benefit, since it is easier to hang themes on individuals if not too much needs to be said about them. Lack of biographical attention may prevent them turning into *prima donnas* and upstaging the narrative.

Another problem about most history (and ancient history in particular) is that the written sources are biased in favour of those who were in a position to produce them. Most of the time, this means the rich and powerful, who left records inscribed on stone or metal. Egypt is more fortunate than some ancient cultures in that the conditions of survival can help us to fill out the picture. We are in a position to know about a character such as the farmer Heqanakhte, because some letters sent by him survived in the dryness of a tomb, whereas most texts written on a flimsy material such as papyrus have perished. Nevertheless, the fact remains that most of Heqanakhte's contemporaries will never be known to us. A similar chance accounts for the petition of the old man Petiese. Many towns of ancient Egypt would have had their Petiese, but we know only one of them. We must use such informants to compensate for what has not survived, but we can never be sure how typical of their society they were. The most detailed account of all is reserved for the five characters of the Serapeum, whose papers are some of the most informative texts to survive from the ancient world. These are fortunate exceptions; otherwise we must resort to the more privileged kings, queens, princes and priests to tell us about the world in which they spent their lives. Even for ancient Egypt, the sources are top-heavy, and this must be faced. For the same reason, we know more about ancient Egyptian men than ancient Egyptian women, but the latter are not all absent from the record, and at least three of them have found their way into these pages.

Those who like their history glamorous can be assured that there are two kings in this volume, as well as one queen who decided that she was a king, and one king's son, albeit an unusual one. After some agonising, but not much, I decided to leave out Akhenaten. The heretic Pharaoh, as he is known, has a habit of unbalancing books on Egyptology, and he needs a study of his own, although there are more than enough works about him in circulation already. However he is handled, there is no way that Akhenaten can fail to dominate a narrative. Instead, he has been smuggled into Chapter 4, and some of his influence will be found lingering in Chapter 5. The same is true of Tutankhamun, who does not need the publicity, and about whose life surprisingly little is known.

It is no coincidence that eight of the twelve characters in this book have links with the site of Saqqara. It is the part of Egypt which is best known to me, and it is one which has produced rich documentation for almost all periods of ancient Egypt. To revisit this place is a pleasure, if only in one's thoughts. Similarly, there is some bias in the book towards the later periods. This too is a personal preference, but one that I hope is justified by the nature of the sources which survive.

The sources which do survive are haphazard. Much of the history of ancient Egypt is pieced together from hieroglyphic inscriptions from tombs or temple sites. These are mostly found on stone surfaces: temple walls, free-standing monumental texts known as stelae, or the obelisks, statues, sarcophagi, and other manifestations of Egyptian religion. The palaces of the Egyptian kings, which were the temples' secular counterparts, are largely lost. Many of the inscriptions are fragmentary, and some contain obscure words or phrases which continue to defy translators. We do not have Nefertiti's diaries or the day-books of the architect who built the Great Pyramid. The chapters on Hatshepsut, Horemheb, Khaemwise, and to some extent Imhotep and Nectanebo, are pieced together from sources which are limited and which, to the modern mind, concentrate excessively on theology. On other occasions documents survive on papyrus, a state of affairs which is made possible by the dry conditions of the Egyptian deserts. Here we are more fortunate, since the subject matter of texts such as these is immediate: it has not been censored by political authorities or by the prejudices of later tradition. The chapters on Heqanakhte the farmer and Petiese the disgruntled scribe are based on documents of this sort. We are fortunate to have them, since so much else has been lost, either to moist conditions, fire, or the appetites of insects. Most remarkable of all are the documents, written either on papyrus or on potsherds, which illustrate the inner lives of the five characters in the final chapter. These are truly remarkable, but here too we can only speculate on what we will never know.

Estimates of the rate of literacy in ancient Egypt vary, but the prevailing ones argue that only 2 per cent of the population were able to write fully. The texts covered in this book suggest that the true rate was higher than this, but here too we are at the mercy of the evidence, since the illiterate can have left few signs of their existence. However, the availability of a class of professional scribes will have enabled some of these to find their voice.

In addition to twelve accounts of the living, I have allowed a thirteenth character to recur throughout the book. This is the god Osiris, the ancient judge of the netherworld, who created the land of Egypt, and before whom the characters in this book believed that they would appear at the end of their lives. It is for this reason that he features in the title of the book, and he also receives a short epilogue at the end.

CHAPTER ONE

Egypt's Leonardo

Imhotep, c. 2650 BC

The French architect Jean-Philippe Lauer is the doyen of archae-ologists in Egypt, and his career as an Egyptologist covers more than seven decades. In his autobiographical memoir, *Saqqarah, Une Vie*, published in 1988, he records an anecdote which he at-tributes to one of his English friends and colleagues, Cecil Firth. One day in the 1920s or thereabouts, Firth had been taking an im-portant tourist around the sights of Saqqara, one of the more vis-ited areas of Egypt. Their tour took in the main feature of Saqqara, the Step Pyramid. Firth explained to the lady that this monument, the earliest of all the pyramids and in many ways the most inter-esting, had been built in around 2800. 'Excuse me,' said the curi-ous visitor, 'Would that be BC or AD?' 'Well,' came the reply, improvising on all cylinders, 'It's so long ago it's difficult to be sure.'

Archaeologists enjoy stories about tourists and their some-times shaky grasp on the culture they have come distances to gaze at, but there is a basis to the story. The scale of ancient Egyptian history can come as a surprise, even to the best informed. Classic-al sources tell us that Cleopatra went on a cruise along the Nile in 47 BC with Julius Caesar. Caesar and Cleopatra were tourists, in an expansive kind of way, and they may have taken time off from the state barge of the Ptolemies, with its choice of restaurants, Egyptian and Greek, to climb the desert plateau to the west of the city of Memphis, with the intention of visiting the same Step Pyramid. In terms of a pyramid lifetime, this is the equivalent of the day before yesterday, since more years stand between Cleopatra and Djoser, the king for whom the Step Pyramid was built, than separate Cleopatra from ourselves. For Caesar and Cleopatra, Pharaoh Djoser was one of the ancient Egyptians.

There is another way of putting this. There is no ideal criterion for defining when history begins, but one way is to start at the point when a civilisation comes up with a system of writing. The more rebarbative school of dirt-diggers, not to mention the prehistorians, may find this criterion irrelevant and elitist, but it will do for this purpose, since it is easy to measure. At the moment of counting, writing began in Mesopotamia, or what is now southern Iraq, in about 3200 BC. Egypt followed quickly on to the scene, and recent discoveries suggest that there were rudimentary writing-schemes in use among the governing elite by 3100, if not earlier. Using this time scale, we can say that fifty-two centuries separate the beginning of Egyptian civilisation from the present day. The history of ancient Egypt is conventionally divided into dynasties, and thirty such dynasties occupy the period between the beginning of Pharaonic kingship and the arrival of Alexander the Great in the country in 332 BC. However, the successors of Alexander the Great, all of whom went under the dynastic name Ptolemy, also used the title Pharaoh, as did the Roman emperors who followed them. There were still Pharaohs after the transfer of the Roman capital to Constantinople and the decision to allow freedom of worship to Christianity, and we can find inscriptions in hieroglyphic, put up by emperors such as Constantius II (AD 337–361), who were Christian, at least on paper, and yet were content to be seen in Egypt worshipping an extremely pagan sacred animal. Texts of this sort bring us down to the middle of the fourth century AD. Given such an afterlife for Egyptian civilisation, we can say that, of the fifty-two centuries which we can define as history, there was a Pharaoh on the throne of Egypt for thirty-six of them. Thirty-six out of fifty-two centuries is almost the equivalent of seven-tenths of the span of recorded events, and we blithely call this ancient Egypt.

The appearance of writing in Egypt has been pushed back by the discovery of inscribed labels in one of the earliest monumental tombs at Abydos, a site in Upper Egypt. It may be that this tomb, which predates the First Dynasty by fifty or a hundred years, is the burial place of one of the chieftains who ruled over much of the south of the country before the beginning of a united state. Mesopotamia may still have the lead over Egypt when it comes to writing, but this Abydos discovery shortens the time-gap to one or two generations. As a result, the most likely explanation is that the Egyptians heard, or saw, that in Mesopotamia scribes were experimenting with pictures to record abstract words as well as concrete objects, and they decided to create a comparable system of their own. All writing arises from the adaptation of pictures to themes which cannot readily be expressed pictorially. Egyptian hieroglyphic and Mesopotamian cuneiform both use pictorial symbols to record phonetic elements as well as ideas, but otherwise the two are distinct. Hieroglyphs are not Mesopotamian signs adapted to a different language; they are new signs adapted to their own language, and they give the impression that they were deliberately created for the purpose.

We will never know who devised Egyptian writing and where, but we do have an idea about the authority which needed such a record-system. This brings us face to face with the most striking feature of early Egypt. Unlike its neighbours, the land of the Nile was a unified state. In the modern world distinct nations are standard, and we tend not to think of this as unusual, but in the ancient world unified political systems were far from being the norm. Mesopotamia started out life as a series of warring city-states, and it is likely that this competitive state of affairs was responsible for much of its technical creativity. The process of unifying Mesopotamia, or Sumer, or Babylonia, or whatever else one calls it, was a complex one, and the frequent change of name, and the political identity which alters with the shifting name, is a reflection of this complexity. Even now, the land of Iraq shows strong regional varieties, and may cease to be a unity when its present form of government breaks up. The Hellenic world was for most of its history a similar patchwork of warring states and shifting alliances. Ancient Egypt was no less complex a society, but it created the first united monarchy in history. It did this 1,000 years before Mesopotamia, and this monarchy lasted, with a few interludes of anarchy, until the coming of Alexander the Great. After this, and under foreign management, Pharaonic Egypt continued down to the death of Cleopatra on 12 August 30 BC, and the shadow of Cleopatra and the Ptolemaic kingdom stretched long and far across the Roman Empire which succeeded her.

What embodied this unified state, and the concept which may well have brought it into being, was the person of the Pharaoh. Here too we are faced with a degree of abstraction which seems far ahead of its time. The theology defining the king of Egypt was complex, and in its full form it is only known from the Sixth Dynasty, several centuries after the emergence of the Egyptian state. Under this system, the king could be seen as the embodiment of various gods, notably Horus, the young sun born from its predecessor which had died the previous night. This predecessor was Osiris, a god who can be thought of as the photographic negative of the sun god: a being who had ruled on earth, been put to death by the machinations of evil and disruptive forces, and who passed into a new life as the light below the earth, ruler and judge of the dead who are in the Underworld.

The notion of the king as a representative of gods is common in the ancient world, but what made the king of Egypt (or Pharaoh, as he was later to be termed) unique was the dual entity which is contained in his most characteristic title. This is the *insib-ya*, or more conventionally the *nesu-biyet* title, which is written with the hieroglyphs for a sedge-plant and a bee respectively. These symbols were the heraldic emblems of Upper and Lower Egypt, and as a result the title is normally rendered 'King of Upper and Lower Egypt', following the translation into Greek which is given on the bilingual Rosetta Stone. However, this can only be a secondary interpretation. What the final part of this title, *biyet*, signifies is the personal, human nature of the king, the aspect which is summed up in the personal name given to him at the moment of birth. The initial part of the compound, *nesu*, corresponds to the divine nature which is within the person, and which is conveyed in the first of the two names normally carried by the king. This prenomen, as it is called, would be given to the king at his accession, and confirmed at the coronation, and it nearly always involves a reference to the sun god himself, the originator of kingship both in heaven and on earth. The divine prenomen and human nomen are written in cartouches, the oval frames which protect them and single them out from the rest of any inscription. On his death, the king was known officially as Osiris the *nesu*, followed by the throne-name (a religious name conferred at the coronation, which defined the new king as an aspect of the sun god). The second name, the one written with the bee-hieroglyph, ceases to exist. On earth, the king had a dual nature, corresponding to the emanation of the divine which was present within his temporal, human, dimension. The latter would grow old, infirm, and die. The former was immortal. Pharaoh was, literally, a god-king.

The implications of this idea for the formation of the Egyptian state were profound, even if the theology which they convey was still in its infancy. The king was literally the incorporation of the newly formed state, and he combined within himself the dual nature, not simply of the human and the divine, but of the two main geographical parts of Egypt, the Delta and the Nile valley to the south of it. Later tradition saw the formation of the Egyptian state as a military conquest by the south over the north. This idea has often been discounted, especially in the iconoclastic days of 'new archaeology' in the 1960s and 1970s, but something of the sort may have occurred. Conquests happen. In reality, the military preponderance of Upper Egypt may have gone hand in hand with philosophical thinking about the nature of kingship, since religion and power tend to be closely linked in the ancient world, a phenomenon which is not entirely absent from the modern.

For one commentator, Michael Rice, the role of the Pharaoh in early Egypt takes the form of a Jungian archetype: to him, the king represents the individuality of a state in which the notion of personal identity had not yet been developed. One does not need to go all the way with this, since it is difficult not to suspect that the individual Egyptians of this period, who were buried by their relatives with expensive grave goods and with all the signs of care and attention that are given to their later descendants, had a very good sense of their own existence. But there is something in the idea: the king of this remote period in time was the embodiment of what made Egypt what it was. He was the sacredness of the land, and one of his titles, a word normally translated as 'Majesty', is properly rendered as incarnation or embodiment.

Even at this early date there were several unusual features which distinguish an ancient Egyptian, and one of these was being dead. The Egyptian cult of the funerary attracted comments from other civilisations throughout most of its history, and it is certainly out of the ordinary run in the ancient world. In Book XI of the *Odyssey*, for example, the eponymous hero wishes to contact the dead Achilles, who is brought back from the Homeric underworld by necromancy. Odysseus cannot resist the temptation to ask his friend what life is like down below. Achilles replies that he would rather be the humblest hired labourer on a poor estate on earth, than king of all the dead. The Babylonian Hades was a similarly gloomy place, and the few references in the Old Testament to an afterlife are not enticing. Life with Osiris, on the other hand, was a place of bliss, at least for the dead king and his associates, and those who passed the judgement in the presence of this awesome god. Exactly who the king's associates were supposed to be at this early stage of Egyptian history is uncertain, but it is not too difficult to imagine that someone who had laboured on the eternal home of the god-king would be allowed some part in his immortality. Such a blanket share in the fortunes of the next world may have extended to those who could secure burial within areas which were close to the tomb of the dead sovereign. This may have amounted to little more than a vague promise, but it is hard to maintain that the relatives of the dead, who buried them in their ever-growing cemeteries on the edge of the deserts, believed that they were headed for extinction. The notion sometimes encountered that in the early dynasties only the Pharaoh was immortal does not tally with the evidence that we have. Osiris was prepared to spend eternity with more Egyptians than this, even if we do not have the full version of his invitation list.

The kings of the First Dynasty were buried at Abydos in Upper Egypt, as were some of the Second. However, as the period develops, there is a growing concentration on the site of Saqqara, on the plateau of the western desert overlooking the city of Memphis. According to Egyptian tradition, the latter was founded by the third king of the First Dynasty, and there is some archaeological evidence, in the form of soundings, to back this up. A series of prestigious tombs was constructed at Saqqara even in the First Dynasty. These tombs, and their contents, were so impressive that their original excavator took them to be royal, but they are now recognised as being the burial-places of high officials. In the Second Dynasty, the sleeping population of the site increases noticeably, and the stage was set for kingly burials proper. However, nothing remains of the superstructures of these royal tombs, and we can say little about the original scenery which stood on this stage. If the superstructures of the private tombs of this period are anything to go by, their royal counterparts will have been marked by large rectangular platforms of mud-brick, with the sort of striated decoration which was characteristic of early palaces. This motif derived from Mesopotamia, as did several other features of the art which emerged in protodynastic Egypt. However, like most of these other features, it was naturalised with impressive ease. This tendency to absorb features from other cultures, but to do it in a way that suggests that the features had been Egyptian all along, is one of the *Leitmotifs* of Egyptian history, and we will encounter it in later chapters.

The Third Dynasty began with the reign of a shadowy king, but he was soon succeeded by the most ambitious ruler of the period, Djoser. There was no false modesty about this monarch; indeed, modesty in any form was not thought a Pharaonic virtue, and there is a noticeable lack of reticence to his principal monument, the Step Pyramid. Even in its modern, and partially reconstructed state, the Step Pyramid has a claim to be the most interesting single monument in Egypt, and it is one of the first. Its date is now thought to be about 2650 BC (it has come down since the days of Cecil Firth and his visitor). Djoser probably inherited the site from his short-reigned predecessor. This does not matter: what is important is that, for the first time, the single platform of adobe which marked the graves of previous rulers was replaced by a series of graduated steps, six in all, forming a mighty staircase into the sky. The idea was an experiment, and realised in tentative stages. Around the pyramid and its enclosure there were pavilions and chapels for the celebration of the king's jubilee. But this is a jubilee intended for eternity. The complex was constructed, not of wood and brick and plaited reeds, but of stone.

An idea of the impact which this architecture had on the mind of later generations can be gained from an unlikely source: tourist graffiti. Ancient Egyptian graffiti are far more pious than their modern equivalents, and are designed to invoke the good intentions of the gods, either towards the person who is buried in the monument, or upon the visitor who has left the record of his journey. Families would make trips to historic monuments, especially on feast days, and a later visitor to one of the pyramids at Dahshur, south of Saqqara, expressed the somewhat gushing hope that heaven would rain frankincense on to the monument of its noble owner. Inscriptions of this sort, always neatly written, are not uncommonly found on the walls of tombs and pyramids which were already centuries old. However, in the middle of the reign of Ramesses II (c. 1245 BC), there came a pilgrim to the site of Saqqara who was convinced that the monument he was visiting marked an innovation in history:

> There came the scribe Nashuyu to the neighbourhood of the pyramid of Teti, beloved of the god Ptah, and the pyramid of Djoser, inventor of stone. And he said to all the gods of the west of Memphis, 'I am in your presence; I am your servant.' Year 34, fourth month of summer, day 24, the day of the festival of Ptah, South of his Wall, lord of Saqqara, when he appears at eventide.

Then he adds at the top, as if in an afterthought, 'Do good, do good, Djoser, inventor of stone, do good to the scribe Nashuyu.'

This is a vivid inscription, but it needs a little comment. The pyramid of Teti is also at Saqqara, situated due east of the Step Pyramid, but it postdates it by almost two centuries, conforming to the somewhat mass-produced style favoured for later royal tombs. On the other hand, Ptah, South of his Wall, is one of the names of the principal god of Memphis. He was the god of crafts-manship and technology, and the day of our scribe's visit was one of his most important festivals. The choice of such an occasion made sense, because the god could be expected to be in a good mood on such a day, but it must also be connected with the un-usual epithet that our writer reserves for King Djoser. 'Inventor of stone' is a unique phrase in Egyptian, and it implies not merely that the writer was capable of conceiving the idea of a technologic-al breakthrough, but that he knew that one had taken place in precisely this reign. Djoser, in the view of this pious scribe, had brought about a new type of architecture.

There is a tendency in the history of science to over-simplify technological advances, and to represent them as happening out of the blue. Stone as such was not invented by anyone, except pos-sibly the Supreme Architect of the Universe; it was there in profu-sion in the desert cliffs on either side of the Nile valley, which is in geological terms a canyon. There had been sporadic use of stone, in the royal tombs at Abydos and one or two prestigious sites else-where. Some way to the west of the Step Pyramid there is a large oblong compound, surrounded by stone walls, known nowadays in Arabic as the Gisr el-Mudir ('The boss's dyke'). Its purpose is unknown, but recent work on this mysterious building suggests that it dates to the end of the Second Dynasty, perhaps ten or twenty years before Djoser. Egyptian rulers were experimenting with stone even at this date, but all these earlier constructions consist of plane blocks and surfaces, whether floors, lintels, or walls. What Djoser did was to treat stone as if it were a plastic medium, and this is what the scribe Nashuyu is telling us.

Nashuyu has also omitted another detail, and this is more sur-prising. Egyptian culture valued writing, and reverence for the scribe permeated its intellectual life. Works of wisdom and man-uals of ethics were ascribed to great thinkers of the past, some-times correctly, at other times by the kind of well-meaning but false

Base of a statue of King Djoser, featuring the king's throne-name accompanied by the name and titles of his architect, Imhotep. Found by the Step Pyramid complex at Saqqara.

attributions which go under the name pseudepigrapha. Old-Kingdom sages such as Hardedef, Kagemni and Kaires were familiar to educated Egyptians, and it is difficult to imagine that our Nashuyu, a man who was happy to coin phrases about invention, had not heard of the most famous sage of all. According to tradition, Djoser owed his monument, and much else that was original in his reign, to the genius of his chief adviser, Imhotep. We know that this man existed from contemporary sources, although we learn little else from them. A statue-base was found in 1926 during clearance work at the Step Pyramid bearing his name, which is the Egyptian for 'The one who has come in peace', or more simply 'Welcome'. There has rarely been a culture which was more obsessed with titles than ancient Egypt, and this inscription does not disappoint:

> The chancellor of the king of Lower Egypt, the first after the king of Upper Egypt, administrator of the great palace, hereditary lord, Greatest of Seers, Imhotep, the builder, the sculptor, the maker of stone vases.

'Greatest of Seers' was the ceremonial description of the high priest of the sun-cult at Heliopolis, the sacred city which lay some twenty-five miles to the north-east of Memphis. The style of this inscription suggests strongly that it dates to the reign of Djoser himself, whose name is also featured on it. It stresses the versatility of Imhotep, even in his own lifetime, and the comparison with Leonardo da Vinci, which is sometimes made by Egyptologists, is not unjustified. In addition, Imhotep's name was found in the mid-1950s, written in ink on the girdle-wall of the unfinished pyramid of Sekhemkhet, Djoser's successor, which is nearby at Saqqara. This implies that Imhotep outlived his royal patron and found favour, as well as scope for his talents, under the subsequent reign. The Leonardo of ancient Egypt was real, and is not a later fiction.

It may be that the writer of our thirteenth-century graffito lived in a period when the popularity of Imhotep was going through a low. A song, roughly contemporary with our scribe, survives written on papyrus, where it is put into the mouth of a harpist performing at a party. It is evocatively said to be from the tomb of a long-dead king. Harpists' songs of this type tend to be melancholy (they were probably recited at dinner parties at the point when intoxication was entering the maudlin stage. Herodotus later records how at similar moments a miniature coffin would be handed round the party guests, with the instruction to enjoy what time was left). Whatever the occasion, our world-weary harpist sings:

> Well is it with this good prince; the kind destiny has come to pass.
> Bodies pass away and others remain, since the time of those who
>   were before ...
> I have heard the discourses of Imhotep and Hardedef, whose words
>   men quote in full. Where are their habitations now?
> Their walls are destroyed, their habitations are no more, as if they
>   had never been.

By 'habitations' the singer undoubtedly means tombs; mere houses would have passed away in the year-by-year interaction between mud-brick and the annual flooding of the river, and no one would expect otherwise. Imhotep's tomb, which was meant to be his eternal abode, was lost by this time, and it may be that much of the tradition about him was lost too. But even our harpist had read the writings of Imhotep, so he must have remained on the curriculum, and it is likely that the scribe Nashuyu knew about him too. What the pious scribe was hoping in his graffito was to attract the favour of the kings themselves, who were buried out in the western desert. They were gods, like Ptah the patron of craftsmen, and they were in a position to further the career of those who called for their aid, especially when they had just put in a respectful visit. For Nashuyu, Imhotep was not a god, but a writer of maxims he had heard at school.

Later tradition judged differently. Manetho, an Egyptian priest who wrote in the third century BC for the Greek rulers who had taken over his country, records in his *History*, a work which has come down to us only in fragments, several details about the Imhotep of his own day:

> Tosorthros [Djoser], reigned twenty-nine years, in whose time was
> Imouthes [Imhotep], who is equated by the Egyptians with
> Asklepios because of his medical skill and his invention of building
> with hewn stone; also for the excellence of his writings.

Nothing could be clearer. If anything, the supposed versatility of Imhotep now surpasses that of Leonardo, as does his status. In texts from the Late Period, the architect of the Step Pyramid is regularly referred to as 'Imhotep the great, son of Ptah, the great god'. In Greek terms he is Asklepios, the god of medicine, a deity who had links with the human world as well as the divine. He had his own temples, not merely in Memphis but in the southern capital, Thebes, and he has now become the offspring of the god who was invoked by the scribe Nashuyu. His father may have been divine, but in this tradition his mother, Khereduankh, kept her human status. Deification of wise men can also be seen in the Greek world, and some have detected Greek influence in the cult of Imhotep. However, the transition from mortal to god seems to have taken place too early for this, and it may even be that the influence went the other way. There are hints of Imhotep's divinity even in the Ramesside period, not long after Nashuyu wrote his graffito. By the Twenty-sixth Dynasty (c. 600 BC) the Egyptians were restoring the Step Pyramid, adding a new entrance to a monument which was already 2,000 years old, and at some point they also unearthed Imhotep's tomb. This was reconstituted as his principal sanctuary, and by Hellenistic and Roman times it had achieved fame throughout much of the Mediterranean as the Asklepieion of Memphis. Earlier in this chapter we imagined Caesar and Cleopatra visiting Saqqara to see the Step Pyramid. What is more likely is that they came to the site to see the shrine of the Egyptian Asklepios. Imhotep acquired a reputation for helping women to conceive, and this is what Cleopatra did during her voyage along the Nile. The focal point of the Asklepieion was the cult statue, showing the deified genius seated with a roll of papyrus on his knees, on which hieroglyphs were carved. Arabic writers of the ninth and tenth centuries describe a similar statue, in a cavern somewhere at Saqqara. In these late, almost folkloric, accounts the temple has become the prison where Pharaoh confined Joseph: a fine example of the way that pagan ideas can survive by weaving themselves into other traditions. Legends about Joseph and his prison continue in the area to this day.

Late-Period Saqqara was the seat of a range of cults and temples, mainly devoted to animals, a feature of Egyptian religion which has puzzled ancient as well as modern observers. Some of these cults we will meet later, but Imhotep is as good a man as any to make the introductions. First on the scene came the sacred Apis bulls, who had a catacomb all to themselves. This is well known to modern visitors as the Serapeum, although this was strictly the name of the Apis's temple above ground. To the north of the site rose a temple devoted to the mother of the Apis, who, by a form of assimilation which resembles divine cronyism, was equated with the goddess Isis. According to one tradition the cow in question was made pregnant by a flash of lightning, and the priests, on the death of one Apis, searched the length of the country for a new-born calf with all the right markings, a procedure which in some ways is reminiscent of the cult of the Dalai Lama. The mothers of the Apis bulls had their catacomb too, and they were joined in death by a colony of sacred baboons, who lived in one of the temples in the valley and went up to the plateau of Saqqara to be buried, whereupon they turned into a corporate entity known as Osiris the Baboon.

There were hawks, sacred to the royal god Horus, and ibises, the bird of Thoth, god of the moon, calendars and learning. At the eastern edge of the plateau, looking out over Memphis at the end of the sacred way that ran from the Serapeum, was a huge temple platform devoted to the gods of cats and dogs. There were other cults too, and the place must have grown to resemble a mummified menagerie. Strange as it may seem, Imhotep would have found good company in such a maze of cults. If the Apis bulls were a little heavy for his taste, he could spend eternity talking wisdom to the ibises and the cats, and most of his days were kept busy listening to the prayers of pilgrims who had made their way to his shrine in the hope that he would cure them of their sufferings. He could appear in dreams, or in some types of visions, and the priests of his cult were skilled at suggesting medicines or other courses of treatment. A pilgrim who had made the effort to attend Imhotep's shrine, who went through the processes necessary to induce a dream of the god, and who left with a convincing-enough prescription to cure his ills, might well have decided that Imhotep was someone who lived up to his promises. Even if the pilgrim later died, he had at least seen one of the great gods of Egypt, who had once been on earth like him.

Beginning in the middle of the 1960s, the Egypt Exploration Society of London explored the plateau of Saqqara, looking for the tomb of Imhotep. These excavations were led by W. B. Emery, who was hoping to crown a highly successful career as an Egyptologist by discovering the father of architecture. Even scholars who are drawn to this sort of thing can sympathise with Emery's exasperation with finding two million mummified ibises, several hundred thousand falcons, and the powdered remains of hundreds of baboons, macaques, and other such fauna. Emery's exasperation was tempered by the discovery of thousands of statues in stone or bronze, many of exquisite workmanship. These were mainly ex-votos from the temples of Late-Period Saqqara. There were also hundreds of texts written on papyrus or potsherds, including a notice to troops, written in Greek, issued by one of the generals of Alexander the Great. But there was to be no Imhotep. During one of these seasons a Japanese airline issued an elegant booklet entitled *Cities of the World*; each entry was accompanied by maps, taxi fares and similar items, and a list of things to see. Japanese visitors to Cairo were urged to flock to Saqqara and see the newly discovered tomb of Imhotep. It is to be hoped that Emery never saw this booklet.

Emery died in 1971, and the excavations at Saqqara were taken over by two of his colleagues in University College London, H. S. Smith and G. T. Martin. Their discoveries have added much to our knowledge of one of the most remarkable sites in Egypt. Some of the texts recovered from the area make mention of Imhotep the great, son of Ptah. This is not surprising, since he was one of the principal gods of the place. But of his tomb, and of the shrine which grew up in and around it two millennia after his death, there is nothing. It is somewhere under the sands of Saqqara, but the deified architect continues to elude us. The sanctuary was

The Step Pyramid at Saqqara. Reconstruction of the entrance corridor, as designed by Imhotep, c. 2650 BC.

probably plundered at the end of antiquity, during or after the decline of paganism, since there are statues and fragmentary inscriptions which certainly come from it. The place may even have been rediscovered in relatively modern times, but if so no record of this has been found. Imhotep will sleep a while longer.

The rediscovery even of the remains of the Asklepieion would be of prime importance, but it is not essential in order to appreciate the achievement of the man to whom it was dedicated. For this it is only necessary to walk over the plateau and enter the compound of the Step Pyramid. It is not so much the size of the monument, although books about pyramids tend to emphasise this sort of thing. The point is that Imhotep was aware of the setting, which is nothing less than the backdrop of the Sahara desert. In such a context, anything small runs the risk of appearing trivial or irrelevant. It is essentially a question of proportion, and the way in which even this mighty staircase to the sky has been made to look naturally sited. In addition, there is the complex which the architect designed to surround the pyramid, and to which it serves as a focus. Empty space is as much a factor in the design as solid stone. The way that light permeates the entrance colonnade, the re-creation in the limestone ceiling of the original wooden logs which would have roofed a palace, the reed-columns translated into the new medium, all are part of an ambitious and meticulous design. This is not building, an activity which had already been done in Egypt for centuries; it is architecture. The designer is unsure how much stress stone can take, so he keeps the blocks small, and decides to bolster some of his columns with buttresses, but one can almost sense his confidence growing as the visitor steps beyond the entrance corridor into the main courtyard. The architect incorporates heraldic elements into his chapels: column-capitals of lotus or papyrus, the emblems of the two halves of the country, and a frieze of cobra heads. But it is remarkable how understated these decorative elements are. After this modesty, the strength of the pyramid, with its chapel on the north side from which a statue of Djoser looks confidently into the heaven, comes as the perfect finale to the entire work. The 'inventor of stone' – who is Imhotep, rather than his royal patron – was an artist of genius.

CHAPTER TWO

A Farmer's Problems

Heqanakhte, c. 1950 BC

We know something about Imhotep, because he was able and successful, and because a rich vein of tradition grew up about him. We would like to know more, but there is no doubting that he was famous, in life and after it. No traditions formed themselves around our second character. He was uneducated, and lived a life that was not exactly plentiful, although he may have been better off than some of his contemporaries. When he died he left a memory of himself with the members of his family, and some of the neighbours, though we will see that this memory was mixed. There are no statues of him, and no tomb, as far as we know. Even if there were, it would tell us very little. When those who remembered him went to Osiris, all knowledge of him faded. But the written word, which allowed our harpist to recall the discourses of the wise men of the past, has enabled us to learn something about this obscure and in some ways unwise character, and what there is to know is revealing. He was a peasant-farmer, whose name was Heqanakhte, and he lived his years towards the end of the Eleventh Dynasty, some 600 years after Imhotep.

One day, around the year 1950 BC, a man was sitting in the corner of the courtyard of a tomb overlooking the west bank of Thebes, the southern Egyptian city which corresponds to modern

One of the original letters of the farmer Heqanakhte, now in the Metropolitan Museum of Art, New York. The script is the cursive form of hieroglyphs, known as hieratic.

Luxor. His name was Merisu, and he was reading a letter from his father. His feelings on reading letters from this source can be reconstructed from their contents, and it may have been at this point that he gathered several of the letters he had received, screwed them into a ball, and threw them away. One of these letters was never opened. It was addressed to a third party, but Merisu never sent it on. The letters became sealed in the filling of one of the shafts of the tomb, and there they were discovered by an American expedition in 1921–2. They are now in the Metropolitan Museum of Art, New York.

The tomb belonged to an official named Ipi, and this man was the *vizier* of the ruler Mentuhotpe II. Since the tomb was found sealed and intact, it follows that the letters date to this time. Recently, an attempt has been made to re-date them to the middle of the following dynasty, about a century later, on the grounds of the pottery with which they were associated. However, datings based merely on ceramics should be taken with a pinch of salt, and it seems easier to stay with the conventional dating. This has the advantage of keeping the spotlight on Mentuhotpe, who is an unusually interesting figure. At the beginning of this man's reign, he was more of a princeling than a king, since Egypt was still in the state of divided semi-anarchy which had enveloped it after the fall of the Old Kingdom more than a century before. The north of the country was under the control of princes from the state of Heracleopolis in Middle Egypt, and it may have seemed to contemporaries that unity would never return. However, in a decisive battle in or around the thirty-ninth year of his rule (c. 2015 BC), Prince Mentuhotpe succeeded in defeating his northern rivals and reuniting the country. He is essentially the first king of the Middle Kingdom, and was honoured as such in later tradition. During the battle, sixty of Mentuhotpe's choicest soldiers were killed, and they were given the equivalent of a state funeral high in the cliffs of Deir el-Bahri, on the west bank overlooking the town of Thebes.

Here they too were found by the American archaeologists, in March 1923. The soldiers died either as a result of arrow-shots or of heavy objects such as stones, thrown from above. This suggests that they had been taking part in a siege. One skull showed the marks of damage by vultures, so that it must have been some time before the bodies could be recovered.

At the foot of the same cliffs, not far from the tomb of Ipi where our letters were found, arose Mentuhotpe's own monument, a terraced temple of unprecedented design, richly decorated, which incorporated the tomb of several of his consorts, and presumably that of the king himself. There was also an underground cenotaph containing a statue of the ruler, which is another strange feature of this mortuary temple. Heqanakhte's name means 'The ruler is mighty', and this may be a nod in the direction of Mentuhotpe, or one of his colleagues in the dynasty.

Thebes in the Old Kingdom had been a one-donkey town, and it cannot have been any more impressive when Mentuhotpe became its prince. But ambition is a quality which cannot be measured in donkeys, and Thebes was destined for greatness. So too was its god, a deity called Amun. Amun's career was to take him to the head of the pantheon of an entire empire, but his origins, like that of his home town, are decidedly dim. His name, perhaps not inappropriately, means 'The Hidden One'. He is not mentioned in the religious literature of the Old Kingdom, and the original protector of Thebes, inasmuch as it can be said to have one, was a falcon-headed war god known as Montu. Some of Amun's iconography is borrowed from this god, but several of his other features are drafted in from another god of the region, the ithyphallic fertility deity known as Min. Later, keen theological minds got to work on the origins of Amun, and managed to insert him into a scheme known as the Ogdoad of Hermopolis. This theological system involved a creator god, and four dual aspects of the original void from which the universe was made; these are the

The god Amun, here shown in the great temple of Osiris at Abydos, receiving offerings from Pharaoh Seti I, c. 1300 BC. By this time the god was at the height of his imperial splendour.

male and female counterparts of timelessness, darkness, invisibility and something which can be translated 'firmament'. Amun was grafted on to this scheme, and the stage was set for him to become the lord of lords *par excellence*, incorporating the aspects of the principal gods of Egypt, most of whom had existed long before this upstart from the provinces. Amun may well be the first example of a god designed by a committee. (The later Graeco-Egyptian composite, Serapis of Alexandria, is a similar creation, which shows that such a thing could be done in the ancient world.) Amun, in upwardly mobile style, got rid of his first wife, a goddess named Wosret, who was the theological equivalent of the girl next door. Instead, he contracted an alliance with one of the most distinguished ladies in the land, the goddess Mut, the embodiment of motherhood. Like her husband, this goddess was somewhat bland in essence, and this made the pair ideal for usurping the roles of more defined, and therefore more limited, rivals. A less cynical school of thought holds that there was no divorce, and that Wosret and Mut are the same goddess going under different names, but if so, we are still dealing with an attempt to upgrade the original product.

Most of this lay in the future, and the first inklings of the cult of Amun have a human touch to them. The deserts on either side of the Nile valley have different characters. On the west, the Sahara is sandy and mostly flat, whereas the Arabian range on the east is rocky and at times mountainous. Somewhere south of modern Luxor, the Nile takes a turn to the right, as if to head for the Red Sea, departing from its normal channel, which is a dried-up bed known nowadays as the Wadi Karnak. Finally the cliffs of the Arabian desert prove too much for the river, which laboriously winds its way back, sometimes heading due south in order to go north, until it rejoins its main channel in the neighbourhood of Nag Hammadi. The result of this waywardness, which is known as the Qena Bend, is that, in the latitude of Luxor, the high cliffs which are supposed to be part of the eastern desert appear on the western side of the river. These are the famous Theban Hills, behind which lies the Valley of the Kings.

The cliffs on the west bank are capped by a natural peak, which happens to resemble a pyramid. Here, in later times, was thought to be the home of a cobra goddess known as Mertseger, 'She who loves the silence'. In the middle of summer in the closing years of the third millennium BC, the priests of the newfangled god Amun made their way up to this peak in order to look out for their divine employer. There they left graffiti recording their observations, and it is here for the first time that the name Amun is found. Amun, or rather his cult-statue, had formed the habit of sailing in his sacred bark across the river to visit the mortuary temple of Prince Mentuhotpe, the founder of the fortunes of Thebes. This occasion, known as the Festival of the Valley after the bay of Deir el-Bahri where Mentuhotpe's temple is situated, was celebrated down to the end of the New Kingdom, when the number of royal mortuary temples that the god needed to visit extended to something like thirty. The festival was still a feature of Roman Egypt, and gave its name to the month in the summer when it was held. This month, under the name Paoni or Baouneh, is still part of the Coptic calendar used in Egypt.

The First Intermediate Period which Prince Mentuhotpe brought to an end is sometimes described as a period of democratisation. This is an exaggeration, and not much of a clarification either, but there is no doubt that the breakdown of the centralised order which had been the mark of the Old Kingdom had painful consequences. For much of the time there was civil war, and increased suspicion throughout the land. Old hierarchies could no longer command automatic respect. The literature of the Middle Kingdom which follows the period of Mentuhotpe and Heqanakhte has an introverted and somewhat sombre tone, compared with what has survived from the earlier dynasties, and there are frequent references to a quality which might be translated as eloquence, persuasiveness, or even propaganda. The state, which had seemed divinely sanctioned, had collapsed, and constant vigilance was necessary if it were not to collapse again. In this less certain world, men needed to be won over. One king of this troubled time is represented in a didactic work, which admittedly survives only in later copies, accepting guilt for faults committed in his reign, and reflecting on the fact that the gods weigh men's deeds when judging them. The colleagues of Mentuhotpe's slain soldiers may have felt that their contribution to the rise of the new regime was as valuable as anyone's. State funerals for their friends were unlikely to be all that they expected in return.

In the light of this, we should turn to a text which appears in the First Intermediate Period, and which was occasionally written on coffins (without the ubiquitous death industry of ancient Egypt, our knowledge would be seriously depleted). It is a speech put into the mouth of a creator god, who is not equated with any of the major gods of Egypt but is set aside by the use of the term 'He whose names are hidden'. He is also referred to by a title normally translated as 'Lord of the Universe', or more literally 'Lord to the Limit'.

Words spoken by Him whose names are hidden. The Lord of the Universe says in the presence of those who still the tempest, at the time when the conclave sets sail, 'Proceed in peace. I shall recall to you four good deeds that my heart devised when I was in the coils of the serpent, in order to overcome evil. I did four deeds within the portals of the horizon. I made the four winds, that every man might breathe, wherever he may be. That is one deed. I made the great inundation, that the bereft might share in it like the great. That is one deed. I made every man like his fellow; I did not command them to do evil, but it was their own hearts which overthrew what I devised. That is one deed. I made their hearts cease from ignoring the West [i.e., death], so that offerings might be made to the gods of the nomes [i.e., the provinces]. That too is one deed. I created the gods from my sweat, and men are the tears of my eye ... Life is mine; I am its lord, and the sceptre will not be wrested from my hand.'

The original makes neat use of the fact that the Egyptian words for 'men' and 'tears' were similar. The belief that the human race is the product of tears resurfaces more than 2,000 years later under biblical influence, when it becomes one of the themes of Egyptian gnosticism. The notion of evil as the result of wilful disobedience is also reminiscent of the Old Testament, although the idea that death is part of the creator's original plan is not. These are moving ideas, but it is no coincidence that this expression of egalitarianism falls out of circulation with the establishment of the new regime: texts like this do not sit easily with the need to maintain hierarchy. Some of its spirit remained, and the idea that kings and governments were morally accountable recurs more than once in the literature of the Middle Kingdom, but in general utopianism is not a feature of Egyptian society, in the Twelfth Dynasty or later.

This unsettled period may have bred theoretical notions of human equality, but in practice what it inculcated was self-reliance. This is a theme which runs through the correspondence of the farmer Heqanakhte, and it is time to concentrate on this character. He moves in a milieu which is far from the royal court, provincial though this court continued to be, and it is noticeable that his letters make no mention of the god Amun. We have described him as a farmer, and this is certainly true, but at some point he acquired the job of ka-servant for the tomb of Ipi where the letters were found. The duties of a ka-priest were to attend to the cult of the dead man's soul, and to keep an eye on the state of the tomb, or at least the public chapels it contained. These duties were relatively light, and they seem in practice to have been carried out by Merisu, the eldest son, during the father's frequent absences from Thebes.

Whoever did the actual work, the extra income provided by this pious moonlighting would have meant the difference between breaking even at the end of the harvest and having a little to spare. The father's letters date to the reign of the king who succeeded Prince Mentuhotpe. They are well written, probably because they were dictated to a public scribe who would have sat by the temple gate and waited for his clients to open their cares and their wallets. Heqanakhte himself may have been illiterate, although the post of ka-servant may have spurred him to a reading acquaintance with the language. (With a complex script such as hieroglyphic, it is possible to build up a reading knowledge, especially of texts which end up being recited from memory, without gaining the ability to write new material for oneself.) However, if the letters were dictated, they vividly reproduce the character of the sender. He is advanced in years, a keen haggler and spotter of opportunities, a busybody, and someone who cannot resist meddling and cajoling while changing his mind at the same time. He is also repetitive, and has a habit of haranguing the recipient with short sentences beginning 'Look'. The frustration of Merisu and most of the rest of this browbeaten family is easy to imagine.

The family's land lay in a place named Nebsoyet, somewhere in the neighbourhood of Thebes, but there was also a subsidiary plot in another village, Perha'a, which was rented. In the house in Nebsoyet we must imagine Merisu and his four brothers, the youngest of whom is a boy named Sneferu. Although we do not have Sneferu's own version of events, it is clear that the lad is his father's favourite, and a spoilt brat. Then there is Heqanakhte's mother, who must have been a lady of considerable years, and a female relative named Hotepet, who for some reason is not on good terms with Merisu. In a cramped house in a village such bad feeling must have been a source of tension, but the most explosive material attaches itself to a third woman, Iutenheb. Iutenheb is Heqanakhte's new wife, and she is much younger than her husband. She may even be younger than Merisu. From this it is clear that, if it were not for the subtropical climate of Egypt which encouraged people to spend most of their time out of the house,

An agricultural scene from the tomb of Ity at Gebelein, south of Luxor. A donkey
ferries baskets of grain to a granary while domesticated antelopes feed
nonchalantly. The provincial, almost naive scene is typical of the period when the
Heqanakhte letters were written. The scene is now in the Museo Egizio, Turin.

there would have been serious trouble in Heqanakhte's home, and
perhaps in the rest of Nebsoyet as well. To this day, Egyptian vil-
lages are rich sources of domestic violence, which can extend to
murder, and to blood feuds which span generations. In addition
to the members of Heqanakhte's family, there are numerous
hangers-on, a feature which is typical of ancient Egypt at all
periods.

The tone of Heqanakhte's language is clear from the way that
he begins one of his longer tirades. This letter was written in mid-
summer, shortly after the head of the household had left on a business trip to somewhere in the north:

A message from the *ka*-priest Heqanakhte to Merisu. Whatever can be inundated on our land, *you* are the one who ploughs it. A warning to all my people, and to you! Listen, I consider you responsible for it. Put your back into ploughing, do your utmost; look after my seed corn, look after all my property. See, I consider you responsible for it; take great care with all my property!

A similar sense of urgency can be found in another letter:

Take great care! Hoe all my land, sieve with the sieve, hack with your noses into the work. Look, if they are diligent god will be thanked for you and I will not have to make things hard for you.

Elsewhere Heqanakhte resorts to gnomic utterances in an attempt to make his point, as when he wistfully concludes, 'Look, this is not the year for a man to be slack for his master, his father, or his brother.' In the last case, one suspects that the three categories of people he lists are all descriptions of himself.

These extracts are typical of the old man in his more ingratiating mode, although it is interesting to note that his references to his elderly mother are invariably respectful. One wonders what she must have been like. One of Heqanakhte's more subtle ploys is to anticipate complaints from his family by contrasting their comfort with his own suffering. He never loses an opportunity to point out that he is making sacrifices so that they do not lack for anything:

Now, what do you mean by having Sihathor [the second son, who acted as a go-between] coming to me with old, dried-out, northern barley from Memphis, instead of giving me ten sacks of good, new barley? Fine – you're happy, eating good new barley while I'm GOING WITHOUT. Isn't that so? Your ship has come in for you, when in fact you do nothing but evil. If you had sent me the old barley simply to keep the new barley intact, what could I have said, [except] 'Well done!'? But since you won't assign me a single bushel from the new barley, I won't assign one to you – for the rest of eternity.

The words that are underlined here are marked in the original with a vertical stroke. Heqanakhte clearly wanted them to be noticed. In another letter he resorts to rhetorical exaggeration to produce the same effect. The family must have complained that they were being kept on short rations:

Bear this in mind: being half alive is better than being plain dead. Listen, you say hunger only about [real] hunger. Look, they are beginning to eat people here. Listen, there is nobody to whom your sorts of rations are given anywhere. So make the most of it until I return. Look, I am going to spend the rest of the summer here.

The family may have taken the last piece of news with unconcealed relief. The economic state of Egypt as it emerged from the internecine struggles of the First Intermediate Period would have been patchy, even desperate in places, but it is unlikely that Heqanakhte's remarks about cannibalism can be taken literally; he is being ghoulish. However, one member who may have regretted the way things were turning out is the favourite youngest child, Sneferu. The tone adopted by Heqanakhte when speaking of this character is completely different from the one he uses with his other sons:

Now if Sneferu really does want to be in charge of those bulls, you must put him in charge of them. He did not want to be with you cultivating, walking up and down, nor did he want to come here with me. Whatever he wants, let him enjoy what he wants. Anyone who rejects these rations, woman or man, should come here to me and live as I live. But there is nobody who has come here to me.

In the first of the two letters quoted here, there is a similar passage:

> Now I have been told that Sneferu doesn't do a thing [this word is damaged, but the meaning is clear]. Take great care of him. Give him a food-allowance. And greet Sneferu – as [Heqanakhte's colleague] Khentechtai does – a thousand times, a million times. Take great care, and write to me ... Take great care of him, and send him to me after the cultivating.

What is going on here is a conflict of interest between Heqanakhte's personal feelings for the Benjamin of his family, and the fact that, in any pre-industrial society, children are economic units. They work the land first and foremost, and to the older members of the family they take the place of pensions and national insurance schemes. Large families are an asset, and childlessness can be a curse. Heqanakhte's favouritism strikes at the well-being of the entire household. Even with this proviso, one has the impression that the tensions within this family can be kept in check. However, it is when we turn to Heqanakhte's new wife, Iutenheb, that the situation becomes dysfunctional. The title Heqanakhte uses to describe this lady literally means 'clothed one', but it is not known what this means: it certainly implies that she was maintained by him, but some editors prefer to translate the word as 'concubine'. Whatever her exact status, the fact remains that she is trouble. In the first letter, there is clearly some sort of friction between the new wife and one of the housemaids:

> Now, be sure to have the maid Senen thrown out of my house – take great care of this – the very day Sihathor returns to you [with this message]. Listen, if she spends one more day in my house ... But it is you who let her do evil to my new wife. Look, why must I scold you? What can she do against you, all five children? Also greet my

mother Ipi a thousand times, a million times, and Hotepet and all
the household. Now, what about this evil treatment of my new
wife? You are taking a liberty. Are you set up alongside me as a
judge? You shall stop – that would be the best thing.

The second letter takes the matter further, showing that the
trouble with the maidservant is only the beginning of the problem. The ubiquitous word 'Look', 'See' or 'Listen' once again
makes its appearance:

Now, you are to send Iutenheb to me. I swear by this man – I mean
Ipi [the deified tomb-owner whose ka-servant Heqanakhte was] –
anyone who commits an abuse against my new wife, he is against
me and I am against him. Look, she is my new wife, and how a new
wife should be treated is well known. Listen, as for anyone who
acts for her as I have acted – would any of you be patient while his
wife is being denounced to him? Shall I be patient? Is there any way
I can be at the same table with you people? Will you not respect
her?

The notion of respect is a familiar sticking-point, especially
among people who have little formal status of their own, but, even
with those who have such status, it can strike at the heart. The precise force of the word here translated 'abuse' is not known, but the
sense is clear enough. The sons have denounced the new wife, or
concubine, to their father. In return, he accuses them of some
kind of assault on her – verbal, physical or even sexual. He may
well have got this information from the lady herself, probably
through the long-suffering intermediary, Sihathor. The situation
is now so fraught that Heqanakhte feels the need to separate the
new wife from his sons. It is clear which party in this dispute he
thinks is in the right, but, by openly taking the side of his new
bride, he is alienating the majority of the household, and the latter

are fit men with minds of their own. This rift may have been a permanent one; at any rate it will have had repercussions. Agatha Christie, whose husband was a well-known archaeologist in the Near East, was shown a translation of the Heqanakhte letters some time after their discovery. She lost no time in writing up the story of this 4,000-year-old family, which she embellished with a murder or two. This was published as her detective novel, *Death Comes as the End*, an afterlife which Heqanakhte can never have imagined for himself, and one of the more intriguing byways of Egyptology.

The world of Heqanakhte is familiar from other texts. It is that of the Middle Eastern peasant at most periods, although in Heqanakhte's case things are exacerbated by the fact that he lived in a time of political transition. The features of such a world are constant: shortages, improvisation, the arbitrariness of fate and secular authority, cynical self-reliance, and the foolishness of hoping for anything more. Within Egypt, such a world finds its fullest expression almost 2,000 years after Heqanakhte, in the collection of sayings which are preserved under the title *The Wisdom of Ankhsheshonq*. This is a miscellany of proverbs and observations about many aspects of Egyptian life, taken from a variety of sources, but there is much in it which Heqanakhte would have recognised readily enough. The supposed author of the *Wisdom* is wrongly imprisoned, and he finds consolation in a lament about the state of the country. 'When the sun god is angry with a land,' he reflects, 'he places the fools in charge of the wise ... When the sun god is angry with a land he makes its washerman the chief of police.' There follows a series of aphorisms, some of which could have come straight from Heqanakhte. 'Drive your son; do not make your servant force him. Do not spare your son work when you can make him do it.' 'Do not say "My land thrives"; never leave off inspecting it ... Do not say "It is summer"; there is winter too.' Occasionally one finds in Ankhsheshonq sentiments which

Heqanakhte might have done well to consider, such as, 'Do not prefer one of your children to another; you do not know which one of them will be kind to you', or, 'Silence is finer than a hasty tongue.' However, it is not generous, nor is it scientific, to moralise to someone out of a text which he can never have seen. In addition, there is a streak of misogyny in *The Wisdom of Ankhsheshonq* which Heqanakhte does not seem to have shared, although a saying such as this might well have struck a chord with him: 'Let your wife see your wealth; do not entrust her with it.'

Outside the culture of Egypt, similar sentiments can be found in the poetry of Hesiod, the crabby farmer from Askra in Boeotia. Hesiod has an interest in mythology which is absent from Heqanakhte, but there is much that the two have in common, and one wonders what would have happened if they had found themselves in the same room. A room which contains both Hesiod and Heqanakhte might not be an easy place, but there is no doubt that the two peasants would have recognised each other as soulmates in the art of spreading gloom while making ends meet. Heqanakhte was cantankerous and opinionated, and he caused grief to those around him, but it is good that we have his letters. They are a small window into a timeless world.

CHAPTER THREE

Gloriana

Queen Hatshepsut, reigned c. 1473–1458 BC

Pharaoh was an icon. Analogies are half-truths, and it is impossible to find a single word which can stand for a complex system of theology which lasted and developed over three millennia. But the term 'icon' comes close to the ancient reality, since an icon, in Eastern Christianity, is a temporal window through which an eternal reality can be glimpsed. The Tsar of Russia could be regarded as a living icon, and so, in much vaguer terms, is the President of the United States. With the king of Egypt, however, the symbolism was quite conscious. Pharaoh was the manifestation of the sun god in time and place; his throne-name contained the name of this god, Re, combined with other elements, often two in number, which corresponded to some of his attributes. The Egyptians regularly referred to their rulers under their throne-names rather than the personal names they had been given at birth, and this continued to be the case after their deaths. This meant that an educated Egyptian had to learn a constantly increasing list of abstract-sounding names, but it did avoid the pedantic numerals after the personal name which we, following the historian Manetho, are obliged to use. Thus the monarch that we know as Amenhotpe, or Amenophis, III, was referred to by contemporaries as Nebma'atre, which means something like 'The sun god is lord of harmonious truth', while Prince Mentuhotpe II of Thebes, under whom Heqanakhte lived, would have been known to the gods as 'The sun god is master of the steering-oar'. The reality behind the king was eternal, although the terms of its manifestation were different each time. A similar system was used for Chinese emperors, almost within living memory, and the notion of the dual body of the sovereign is something which was a feature of the English monarchy, particularly in the late medieval and early modern periods. This is a parallel to which we will return.

Given the fact that the divine essence of the king was unchanging, the personal side of royalty was free to develop much as it liked. Kings grew old and infirm, and finally the human side of their natures died. There was no blueprint for a personal ruler, apart from a general requirement that he ruled in accordance with Ma'at, the principle of morality, justice, or harmonious truth referred to in the previous paragraph. This said, Pharaoh could assume all sorts of characters, and our sources either make this clear, or hint at the nature of the ruler's personality. He could be athletic, like Amenophis II, a ruler who suffered from following a highly successful conqueror who was also his father, or the Nubian Pharaoh Taharqa, who must have been gifted as a runner, since he was able, according to one text, to pace his crack regiment while exercising in the desert. Amasis of the Twenty-sixth Dynasty was a drinker of Stakhanovite capacity, who made a point of being represented as one of the lads in order to maintain his popularity, since he had usurped the throne in a military coup. Pepi II of the Sixth Dynasty is represented in later traditions as walking through the streets of Memphis at night on his way to an assignation with his favourite general. Such behaviour was not approved, but it made no difference to the fact that he was Pharaoh. Contemporary sources do not mention Pepi II's sexual habits, but we have one of his letters, an excited missive about a dancing dwarf which he wrote, at about the age of seven, to an explorer of Africa who had discovered this wonder. Pepi II was very young at the time, but there was already a love of the theatrical in his nature. One king of the Fifth Dynasty was happy to be portrayed in sculpture as a teenager with a first moustache. Other Pharaohs were bores (we will not be able to avoid meeting one in this chapter), although in matters of this sort the message can only be implicit, since Egyptian texts do not make judgements of this sort; nevertheless, boring some of them will have been. There is even a short period in the late fourth century BC when Pharaoh, in this case the son of Alexander the Great and Roxane, was ruling under a legal fiction, since he was dead. This is an interesting variant, but one unlikely to have been common.

Pharaoh could be all sorts of things, but could he be female? Theoretically, the answer to this question was 'yes', since there are creation texts in which the sun god is given female attributes as well as male, but what was possible in an abstract system of philosophy might not have been so welcome in practical politics. According to a scheme which was in circulation by the Nineteenth Dynasty, and which may have applied earlier, there had indeed been female rulers in Egyptian history, but these had reigned at, or very near, the end of the Old and Middle Kingdoms. (The Old-Kingdom queen, Nitocris, attracted considerable legends, and appears prominently in the pages of Herodotus.) Women rulers were possible, therefore, but only at the cost of the breakdown of civilised society. On this line of thinking, female Pharaohs were not natural.

The question of women's rights in ancient Egypt has been much discussed, sometimes tendentiously. Several authors state openly that the country was a matriarchy, with the throne, in particular, passing down over generations through the female line. True matriarchies are extremely rare, and we can be sure that ancient Egypt was not one of them. Pharaoh was Pharaoh because his father was; he was Horus to his predecessor's Osiris.

Akhenaten, the heretic, succeeded his father Amenophis III. Although the full extent of this king's unorthodoxy would not have been clear at the early stage, it would have been known at court that his religious tendencies were suspect. His mother was a commoner, yet this fact is never used against him, presumably because it had no legal force. The status of a particular prince's mother may have helped his case in practice, but this would only have been a secondary part of his claim. However, while the matriarchy idea may be unfounded, no impartial observer can go through an anthology of Egyptian literature or a volume on Egyptian art without coming away with the impression that women did have a relatively high status, and were held in affection as well as respect. Egypt was not a bedouin society, where women are seen as an encumbrance. Instead, the dependence of Egyptian society upon agriculture meant that those who worked the field and tended households were held to be valuable. Egypt was, in many ways, a Mediterranean society, and one in which the most powerful official could be reduced to ineffectualness by a remark from his mother. We have noticed this trait even in someone as outspoken as Heqanakhte, and the title 'mistress of the house', which is regularly given to married women who had no other distinction, is likely to mean what it says: there is no male equivalent. Divorce and inheritance laws, as far as we can reconstruct them, gave women generous treatment, in comparison with most ancient societies and many modern ones. Since children were invaluable, a woman who married and produced offspring, especially if the offspring were male, would have had considerable status, and might have felt that she had not made a bad bargain. Support outside the family structure would have been minimal, even non-existent, but the life of a woman whose husband and sons were comfortably situated would have seemed better than destitute independence. Ancient Egypt was not an ideal place to be a woman, but it was better than many.

The earlier part of the Eighteenth Dynasty is normally called the Tuthmoside period, after the name of its principal rulers. Tuthmosis I (c. 1504–1492 BC, although another reckoning would raise these dates by about twenty-five years) took on the scattered principalities of the Near East and succeeded in carrying his arms over the Euphrates, the river which the Egyptians described as the topsy-turvy one, since it flowed in the opposite direction to their own. He is therefore credited with being the founder of the Egyptian empire in Asia, a concern which occupied much of the foreign policy of the next two centuries. However, this was in the future, and contemporaries may have felt that a show of arms was all that was needed to ensure Egyptian hegemony in the region. A predominate sphere of interest may have been what Tuthmosis I was trying to achieve, and this he did. He was succeeded by a son, Tuthmosis II, which is all that needs to be said about him. As Pharaonic nonentities go, Tuthmosis II can be taken as the paradigm. It is this man's wife who concerns us.

Tuthmosis II was married to his half-sister, Hatshepsut. This was acceptable in Egypt, at least among royalty, and the queens in the Tuthmoside family enjoyed considerable prominence; they too were descended from the dynasty's heroic founder. Distinction of this sort was something best kept in the family. All the same, it is possible that the king was aware of his wife's ambitions. The name Hatshepsut means 'Foremost of the noble ladies', and it had been given, or at least approved, by their joint father, Tuthmosis I. On Tuthmosis II's premature death (c. 1479 BC) the couple had succeeded only in producing a daughter, a princess named Nefrure, and the official heir was a son of the king by one of his minor wives, who was destined to come to the throne, not unpredictably, as Tuthmosis III. Clearly this young boy was in need of a mentor and a regent. His aunt, sweeping aside all talk of bad precedents hundreds of years in the past, felt that there was no one better qualified for this post than herself, and, more importantly, she was able to convince others of this. She and Tuthmosis III were declared coregents. There had been coregencies before, during the Middle Kingdom, and this went some way to glossing over the less conducive fact that one of the partners, in this case the senior in terms of experience of the world, was a woman. In the early years of the joint reign, Hatshepsut is shown dutifully following her partner when he performs religious rituals, but ritual, in the sense of a procedure to which lip-service is paid, is probably the correct word for this sort of scene. It is as if she is testing the political water before taking the decisive plunge. In reality, she was queen of Egypt from the moment of the coronation, and she took the throne-name Ma'atkare, which means 'Truthful harmony [a female concept which was also divine] is the genius of the sun god.' Hatshepsut's reign as Pharaoh had begun, and it would last twenty-two years.

A case can be made for saying that all historical activity depends upon the meanings of words; at the least, any attempt to change history can involve coming up against the language in which that history is expressed. Hatshepsut, aware of this problem, constructs a feminine version of the theology of kingship. The Pharaoh was the manifestation on earth of the male god Horus. Hatshepsut was to be no exception, but the epithets she uses to refer to herself in this way are put into the feminine gender. She calls herself 'the female Horus of fine gold', fine gold (or electrum) being an amalgam of gold with silver which was more valuable than gold at this period. We could loosely translate this title as 'the platinum goddess', although this may be to introduce a touch of Hollywood into things. Hatshepsut, however, would have had no objection to being a screen idol, and perhaps the metaphor is a good one after all. In a similar way, the standard epithet 'his majesty' (literally, if inelegantly, 'his embodiment') is kept by Hatshepsut but the noun and pronoun are turned into their feminine equivalents, as if it were 'her embodimentess'. On

Queen Hatshepsut, in relief from the walls of her temple at Deir el-Bahri. Here the representation has a feminine quality, although the ruler is still depicted with the ceremonial beard of a male Pharaoh.

other occasions she can be described, paradoxically but more conventionally, as 'the king himself'.

There is a resemblance here to the situation in which Queen Elizabeth I of England found herself on her accession, when she adapted the pre-existing doctrine of the dual body of the sovereign for a state of affairs where one of the bodies happened to be female. In her speeches, Elizabeth I made references to the maleness which was somehow inherent in her, and this is not the only point of comparison which these rulers share. Rewriting language in the light of gender is not a post-modernist phenomenon. We do not know whether this was done by Nitocris or her Middle-Kingdom counterpart; at the moment, the first feminist revamping of language is the work of Hatshepsut, or of her advisers. The queen must have approved these changes, however, and we can be sure that they reflect her thinking. In temple scenes, which are by nature conservative, Hatshepsut appears as a purely male figure, even down to the ceremonial beard which distinguished the Pharaoh. In three-dimensional sculpture, on the other hand, she is free to appear as a woman, somewhat conscious of her dignity it is true, but with an unmistakable feminine version of the Tuthmoside profile. Hatshepsut's portraits, like many other things about her, are her own.

Together with the queen's determination to alter religious language goes an acute historical sense. The need to rewrite history in order to accommodate this exceptional woman is seen in the official account of Hatshepsut's accession to the throne. Here she tells us that the choice of her as ruler was made, not by inheritance or popular acclamation, but by an oracle of the god Amun himself. By the middle of the Eighteenth Dynasty the humble origins of Amun had been forgotten, and he was the undisputed head of the Egyptian pantheon, at least in Thebes, the capital city. It is quite possible that an oracle of this sort did pronounce, although not necessarily at the time we are told that it did. This would have been easy for Hatshepsut's supporters to arrange after she had seized power, in a process of divine laundering. What is more important is that the queen cuts out any form of human intermediary, and goes straight for ratification from the supreme god. As Pharaoh, she would have had this ratification as a matter of course, and there would be no need to labour this aspect of things. But Hatshepsut needs to extract everything she can from the theology which underpins Pharaonic rule. The platinum goddess has something in common with Gloriana, the mystical transformation of Elizabeth I, although in Hatshepsut's case the transformation seems to have begun early in her reign.

Determination to set history in context is also seen in one of Hatshepsut's most unusual monuments. In a remote valley in Middle Egypt, some 175 miles south of present-day Cairo, is a rock-cut temple known, when it is known at all, under its classical name Speos Artemidos, or 'Grotto of Artemis'. The Artemis in this particular case was known to the Egyptians as Pakhet ('the Scratcher'), and she took the form of a lioness. Hatshepsut may have felt an affinity with her. On the façade of this temple, which is a very unusual piece of architecture, is a long inscription, designed to glorify the goddess, and to 'record the annals of her [Hatshepsut's] supremacy for ever'. In this inscription Hatshepsut announces one of the preoccupations of her reign, which is nothing less than a remodelling of the whole of Egypt. There are solar metaphors embroidered into the entire text. This is not unusual in Egypt, but it begins a theme which will recur in other compositions of this ruler. She describes herself as predestined since the moment of creation to restore the purity of the temples, and to return to the perfection of the world at its origins. In a modern context this would be called fundamentalism, and this is not an improper way to regard it here. Hatshepsut was not an orthodox ruler, and she needed to appeal to deeply conservative instincts if she were to flourish. Then she adds:

> I raised up what was dismembered, even from the time when the Asiatics were in the midst of the Delta, overthrowing what had been created. They ruled in ignorance of Re [the sun god], and acted not in accordance with divine command, until the reign of my august person.

The reference to dismemberment here recalls the death of Osiris, and by implication the miraculous re-animation which reversed this. The Asiatics of this text are the hated Hyksos, who ruled Lower Egypt from their capital Avaris during the Second Intermediate Period, and were expelled by the Theban princes at the start of the Eighteenth Dynasty. So far so accurate, but there is considerable spin in the second half of the quotation. Hyksos rule was shameful, but it was not godless barbarity, and the Asiatics did not continue in power until the arrival of Hatshepsut. What she is doing here is putting herself at the forefront of an assault on chaos and irreligion, tantamount to a new ordering of the original process of creation. A modern mind would see this as a cynical pose, but it may well have corresponded to Hatshepsut's thinking. The impulse to re-create may have been one of the things that drove her.

Another side which the Egyptian queen shares with her sixteenth-century English counterpart is a lack of military activity. Egyptian Pharaohs were head of the army, and 'widening the borders of Egypt' was rapidly becoming a requirement for New-Kingdom rulers. There is evidence for minor hostilities in Nubia, so there cannot have been a ban on military activity, but there is no escaping the contrast between Hatshepsut's reign and the frantic campaigning of Tuthmosis I and the adult Tuthmosis III. It is an easy option to see this as a deliberate policy, an attempt to introduce a feminine and pacifist note into the politics of the Egyptian empire. However, this is completely at variance with everything we can deduce about Hatshepsut's character, and there have been many examples of female rulers who are more aggressive than men, especially when they feel that they have something to prove. A more likely explanation is that Hatshepsut could not trust the army. The military aristocracy remembered the successes of her father's reign, and this was a demanding legacy. If Hatshepsut were to lead the army into battle in Asia, what would happen if she lost, even if the army were prepared to follow her in the first place? A female commander-in-chief would be the obvious scapegoat for a military defeat. On the other hand, if the army won without her, it might start agitating for more campaigns, and with it a commanding role for her nephew, who would establish a growing power-base the older he became. Military activity was something best avoided for Hatshepsut, as it was for Gloriana.

An unemployed army is a danger, and an expensive danger, and an outlet needs to be found for its energies. This must have been one of the reasons for the famed expedition to Punt, which is probably the best-known event of Hatshepsut's reign, although it is one that tends to be treated in isolation. This voyage of exploration occupied much of the eighth and ninth years of her reign (c. 1473/2 BC). Punt was the fabled home of the frankincense-tree, and it could only be reached by lengthy voyages along the coast of the Red Sea. Its exact location is unknown: the majority of commentators prefer Eritrea or some part of Somalia, but there is still the remote but romantic possibility that it lay further south, even as far as Zanzibar. This expedition clearly struck a chord with Hatshepsut, and it is recorded in meticulous detail on the walls of her funerary temple at Deir el-Bahri, which she built to the north of the resting-place of Prince Mentuhotpe. The art of the Tuthmoside period shows a preference for clear lines and sensitive colouring, and the Punt reliefs are a masterpiece of their kind. They show the departure of the great fleet, the eventual arrival at 'the god's land' (the exotic place at the end of the earth), and the shipping of the produce of Punt: monkeys, gemstones, animal skins, tropical plants, and incense trees in considerable numbers. The expedition was accompanied by artists and scholars, who recorded the flora and fauna of the Red Sea and the African coast. This is an interesting foreshadowing of Napoleon's *savants*, who set out to record ancient Egypt, and it is not an exaggeration to see Hatshepsut's Punt expedition as the beginning of comparative anthropology.

One of the sights which aroused the curiosity of Hatshepsut's sailors and artists was the queen of Punt herself, who appears in the Deir el-Bahri reliefs as a grotesquely obese figure accompanied by a donkey. The touch of bathos here is deliberate, and the contrast with the slim lines of the Queen of Egypt is intentional.

Five ships, laden with produce, returned by sea, but the other part of the expedition made its way overland to the upper Nile, a considerable feat of exploration. The expedition's commander was the chancellor Neshi, and this Walter Raleigh of the ancient world deserves more commemoration than the inscriptions at Deir el-Bahri give him. Hatshepsut doubtless intended to claim the credit for the whole thing, and one suspects that she held forth about it at state banquets for years afterwards. The reasons for the voyage were complex. Apart from gratifying the queen's vanity, it also allowed her to appear as the provider of the exotic, a role which was expected of Egyptian rulers. There was an economic aspect to the affair, since it had the effect of sourcing an extremely valuable product – frankincense – and bringing about the possibility that it could be grown and processed in Egypt, thus cutting out foreign traders. It was certainly a distraction for an otherwise idle army, and it may well have been hugely gratifying. There is no reason to discount the last as a motive for historical events.

The scenes of the expedition are accompanied by a text, which adds, among other things, that a statue of the queen, shipped from Egypt for the purpose, was put up in this distant land. The excitement caused by the whole voyage is shown by something which has not been noted by commentators. Towards the end of the text, there is a list of the produce of Punt: myrrh and resin, terebinth and balsam, giraffe-tails, incense, hounds, apes and monkeys. This list is almost exactly the same as one which occurs in a romance known as the *Tale of the Shipwrecked Sailor*. The *Shipwrecked Sailor* is known to us only from one papyrus, now in St Petersburg, but it seems to date from the Twelfth Dynasty, four or

The graceful terraces of Hatshepsut's masterpiece, the temple at Deir el-Bahri in western Thebes, set against the backdrop of the Theban Hills.

five hundred years before Hatshepsut. It is a tale about a castaway who finds himself on an island, together with an awesome but benign serpent, who turns out to be a magician and a Prospero-like figure. The story has a distinctly miraculous element to it, and the castaway eventually returns to his home, complete with his friends whom he had seen drowned, and the list of precious items. Its inclusion in the text of the Punt reliefs was intended to remind the audience that here was a modern miracle. Under Hatshepsut, fiction was real.

Many of the incense trees were planted in front of the queen's temple at Deir el-Bahri, and the roots of some of these can still be seen. There they perfumed the night air, but this may be all they did, and there is no evidence that frankincense ever became naturalised to Thebes. The Deir el-Bahri temple has been excavated and slowly reconstructed over the past century, and the artist who first copied many of its scenes was a young man named Howard Carter. It was designed with its three terraces set into a bay in the western cliffs, and it is one of the most dramatic, as well as aesthetically satisfying, sights in Egypt. To walk from the Valley of the Kings by the ancient footpath which winds its way over the top of the hillside, and to look down as the terraces come into view, is something which does not fade from the memory. The austere elegance of the carved scenes on the walls, the balance between light and shade (the valley at this point is very exposed to direct light), and the originality of much of its design, make Hatshepsut's temple unique. The idea of terracing was taken from the monument of Prince Mentuhotpe, but Hatshepsut's architects went far beyond this earlier work. Contemporaries may have found the temple too unique for comfort; certainly no attempt to copy it seems to have been made. There are elements to it which seem anachronistic even to us. Textbooks tell us that the Doric column was developed in Greece, around the seventh century BC. The north colonnade of Deir el-Bahri is composed of Doric columns, eight centuries before this, and this is not the earliest example of this style in Egypt, although the use in colonnades may well be new. A section of the temple was devoted to the myth of the divine birth of Hatshepsut, another piece of theology which normal rulers did not need to emphasise. The god Amun conceived the desire to create his divine image on earth, to reveal his greatness and to do his will. He disguised himself as Tuthmosis I, visited this king's wife, and the result of their discreet conversation was Hatshepsut. Amun had given Egypt his image, and it was female. Who was man to set aside what Amun had willed?

Similar reluctance to understate is found in an unusual context, but one that is typical of this ruler. In the sixteenth year of her reign, Hatshepsut set up an inscribed pair of granite obelisks

Queen Hatshepsut as a kneeling Pharaoh, being blessed by the god Amun. Scene carved on the pyramidion, or capstone, of one of the Queen's obelisks at Karnak.

before the great temple of Amun at Karnak, on the east bank opposite Deir el-Bahri. The entire work, from quarrying to erection, took seven months, and this was not the only pair of obelisks Hatshepsut dedicated. In Egyptian theology, obelisks were the embodiment in stone of the first ray of light which created the universe, in other words what cosmologists nowadays describe as the Big Bang. In her obelisk inscriptions, Hatshepsut knows the mind of God. She is present with the creator at the beginning, and shares in his most secret thoughts; she is 'the luminous seed of the almighty one', and she is also 'the fine gold of kings', another reference to electrum, and an interesting anticipation of Cleopatra, who was to give herself the title 'queen of kings'. Nor is this simply a poetic metaphor: electrum was used to coat the upper parts of the obelisks, in order to make the majesty of the god visible, and with it that of his representative. The queen's consciousness of her place in history, and the force of her personality, are clear from extracts such as this:

> Those who shall see my monument in future years, and shall speak
> of what I have done, beware lest you say, 'I know not, I know not
> how this has been done, fashioning a mountain of gold like
> something self-created' ... Nor shall he who hears this say it was a
> boast, but rather, 'How like her this is, how worthy of her father.'

The obelisks were situated in front of a columned hall of Tuthmosis I, and the text claims that it was he who began the obelisk habit. This is true of Karnak, though it is not true of the rest of Egypt. There is no doubting that Hatshepsut is preoccupied with her father. He had been Pharaoh, and this is not unimportant, but it does not account for the number of times that he is mentioned in her inscriptions. The sarcophagus of Tuthmosis I was discovered not in his own tomb, but in his daughter's, where it had been transferred, presumably on her orders. She intended to spend eternity with him. This too is unprecedented. She left her husband, Tuthmosis II, where he had been buried, and her inscriptions scarcely refer to him, although he too had been Pharaoh, and he was the father of her child, Nefrure. Hatshepsut's mother is rarely mentioned, except in the divine birth narratives, where it would have been hard to avoid. The preoccupation with Tuthmosis I may have been mythological, and was certainly political; for Hatshepsut, mythology and politics were intermeshed. But the trait may be personal, since it is found with some other powerful women, though not all. Elizabeth I made a point of interviewing ambassadors beneath a portrait of her father, Henry VIII. Benazir Bhutto made a political platform out of her father's memory, and Anna Freud made an intellectual one out of hers. None of this is abnormal. Did Tuthmosis I ever refer to his daughter as the best man in the dynasty? This is not completely fanciful: among the queen's inscriptions is a reworking, unfortunately very fragmentary, of an episode in her childhood, when her father proclaims her as his heir before the court. This may have happened, although the chances are that Tuthmosis III was given this role. Perhaps Hatshepsut had held the title in the absence of a male claimant. Or could this scene be based on a chance remark to an impressionable girl who never forgot it?

Hatshepsut used the name of her illustrious father for political ends (something she may not have distinguished from her personal feelings), but in practice she needed more than this. Fortunately, we know the way she held on to power. Early in her reign she may have been able to rely on advisers who had served her father or husband, but after this stage almost all her supporters turn out to be new men, people who owed little or nothing to traditional hierarchy or aristocracy. These were people selected by her, who owed their loyalty directly to their royal patron. The advantages to Hatshepsut were twofold: she could choose people according to what she perceived as merit, rather than out of a sense of obligation for favours received, and she could be confident that, if she fell from power, they would too. It was in their vital interests to keep her on the throne. Akhenaten, later in the dynasty, met the same problem with the same tactic, since he too was politically vulnerable. Appointees such as the seal-bearer Nehasi, and Hapusonbe, the High Priest of Amun, were Hatshepsut's men through and through, and this is shown even in the architecture of their tombs, which were situated within viewing distance of the queen's temple, and whose façades copied the terracing of its distinctive design. Even in death, they would be her men. Hatshepsut was no virgin queen, but she was a widow, and it is not difficult to imagine a court where male favourite after male favourite was kept competing for her good will.

There is no doubt that the most successful favourite was her adviser, Senenmut. Senenmut's main theatre of operations is the temple at Deir el-Bahri, where he appears almost as a master of ceremonies. In some of the chapels of this remarkable building there are small niches, where the figure of its designer is shown, worshipping the god Amun along with his royal mistress. These niches would have been hidden behind the doors when they were open, but the gods would have known that they were there, and there can be little doubt that this was done with Hatshepsut's approval. A further sign of Senenmut's exalted status is his appointment as tutor to the queen's daughter, and there are statues surviving which show him crouching, with the head of the little princess peeping out from his knees. An even greater honour was the fact that he was given permission to be buried within the precinct of the temple itself. At some point around the seventh year of the queen's reign Senenmut's mother died, and she too was buried in his tomb within the temple. Senenmut took advantage of the occasion to exhume the body of his father, in order to give him reburial in what had become the family vault. Neither parent has any title worth speaking of, though the

Egyptians, as we have seen, were obsessed with titles. Senenmut's father had been buried in poverty, and it is likely that the queen's right-hand man had been born in an obscure town, perhaps a village, somewhere along the Nile. He owed his career entirely to Hatshepsut. Interestingly, he does not appear to have married, which is unusual in ancient Egypt. Walter Raleigh's career hit a severe obstacle when he dared to marry one of Gloriana's maids. Can something similar have applied at Hatshepsut's court?

Some years ago, in an unfinished tomb in the cliffs above Hatshepsut's temple, a series of graffiti came to light. One of these is an amateurish drawing of Senenmut, but on another wall there is a sketch showing a female Pharaoh submitting passively to the amorous attentions of a male figure. This may be contemporary with the queen's reign, and it could mean that the relationship between Hatshepsut and her closest adviser was rumoured to be more than architectural. But it is difficult to know what to make of such a scene. Strong female rulers tend to attract speculation of this sort, as is shown by the case of Cleopatra and, with more smoke hinting at fire, Catherine the Great. Alternatively, the scene might correspond to a wistful fantasy thought up by someone with time on his hands, and it is always possible that it was composed after Hatshepsut's death, when hostile reaction against her was free to express itself.

Hatshepsut died on the tenth day of the sixth month of her twenty-second year as Pharaoh of Egypt (according to the dating system adopted here, this would be early February, 1458 BC). On the assumption that she was in her teens when she married Tuthmosis II, she would have been in her mid-fifties. Her nephew, Tuthmosis III, who had been kept in decorative obscurity throughout what was supposed to be a joint reign, lost no time in setting out for Syria, where, in a series of seventeen brilliant campaigns, he succeeded in creating a new Egyptian dominion in the Near East. His frustration is easy to comprehend, and it comes as no surprise when he turns to proscribing his aunt's memory. The interesting thing is that he waited for several years before attempting this, perhaps because he needed to bide his time until most of her powerful supporters had gone to join her. He may have remained in awe of her, and might even have had affection for her, being forced to act against her memory only for reasons of state. Whatever the reason, her name began to be erased from monuments, and her obelisks at Karnak were bricked up so that their hieroglyphs could never speak again. She disappears from history, which is one reason why we do not have a Greek version of her name, unlike the Tuthmoses and the Ramessides who survived to be recorded by Manetho. The bodies of many New Kingdom Pharaohs were discovered in the Valley of the Kings, and are now in the Cairo Museum. Either Hatshepsut is not among them, or she is one of the anonymous ones. She is the re-creation of modern Egyptology, which is as it should be. Will she become a feminist icon, a role which she would have understood and might have relished, or will she continue to disconcert historians, as she disconcerted some of her contemporaries?

CHAPTER FOUR

Justice and the Moon King

Horemheb, reigned c. 1323–1295 BC

When His Majesty came to the throne, the temples and the towns of
the gods and goddesses from Elephantine [Aswan, at the First
Cataract] to the marshes of the Delta coast were fallen into decay,
their shrines ruined, reduced to mounds overgrown with thorns.
Their sanctuaries were like something which never existed, and
their precincts were a footpath, for the earth was derelict. The gods
had turned their backs on this land. If an army was sent to Syria to
widen the boundaries of Egypt, there was no victory. If one prayed
to a god to entreat something from him, he would not come, and if
one petitioned any goddess similarly, she would not come. Their
hearts were weary within them, and they annihilated what had been
made.

These lines come from the Restoration Decree of Tutankhamun,
and they describe the consequences of heresy. For seventeen years,
the throne of Egypt had been occupied by Akhenaten, and the religion of the Pharaohs was set aside. Akhenaten, who came to the
throne as Amenophis IV but changed his name along with his religious views, was a genius, but the combination of religious enthu-
siasm and near-absolute power is something that can unbalance
any personality. His portrait-statues, which are unmistakable,

show the face of a visionary and an artist of great imagination, but it is a face which one would not quickly choose to contradict. As is usual in such circumstances, people did not contradict him, but the resentment and opposition which he provoked burst into the open in the years following his death. Akhenaten's religion was an austere form of monotheism, centred on a deity which he termed the Aten, the disc or globe of the sun, who ruled without a rival and without a traditional temple of his own. Akhenaten moved his court to a deserted bay in the eastern cliffs some 200 miles south of modern Cairo, a site which he chose precisely because no other god had been worshipped there. This capital, to which the reformer gave the epithet 'Horizon of the Aten', is known to Egyptologists by a made-up Arabic name, Tell el-Amarna, and the period of Akhenaten and his short-lived successors is regularly referred to as the Amarna period. Little more than 100 years ago, nothing was known of Akhenaten and his religion, and it is more than likely that Cleopatra had never heard of him, since he vanished from the historical record even more completely than Hatshepsut. However, and as if by way of compensation, Akhenaten has become the Freudian, post-modernist, revolutionary and angst-ridden figure which the twentieth century was looking to create, and he and Nefertiti have books, films, and even an opera to themselves.

What caused the contemporary reaction against this exceptional man? An admirer would say that the religious ideas which he tried to implant were too lofty for the ancients to contemplate, and the Egyptians were not ready for such a man. A sceptic could respond by saying that all religious fanatics are unbearable, and the Egyptians showed a healthy dislike for the Aten and his self-appointed intermediary; after all, Akhenaten's artists portrayed him with a distorted body, and it would not be difficult to believe that he had a distorted mind as well. In addition, Nefertiti, his consort, can be seen as one of the more manipulative First Ladies

The heretic Pharaoh Akhenaten and his wife, Nefertiti, making offerings to the new
god, the Aten, who is shown as a solar disc with outstretched arms. From a relief
found at Amarna, Akhenaten's capital. Now in the Cairo Museum.

in Egyptian history, since she came close to being a joint ruler with
her husband and may have become so in doctrine as well as in
practice. The second of these two interpretations may well be
close to what Akhenaten's enemies believed, but the first is much

more difficult to sustain. Akhenaten's religion was monotheistic, but such an idea was not unusual in ancient Egypt, and we have met a good example in the text put into the mouth of the creator god quoted on p.30. Expressions such as 'god' or 'the god' (once the Egyptian language acquired a definite article) were not unusual. As is common with religious expressions, they could be used on several levels at once, to refer either to the particular god of a situation or a locality, or to distinguish the world of the divine as opposed to the world of men and women, or to the reigning king as a source of justice and morality, or as the equivalent of universal terms such as Lord of the Universe. A monotheistic tendency was present in Egyptian religion, and some Egyptians might well have answered the question, 'Do you think that there is one principle behind the multiplicity of gods you worship?' with an affirmative. In Sais in the Delta, for example, there was a virgin goddess who gave birth to the sun at the beginning of time by some form of parthenogenesis. At Esna in Upper Egypt the same goddess inhabits a temple with the god Chnum, and the two produce a very different child of their own. At Aswan, the same god has a wife who was originally Nubian, and they have a daughter, a rather fetching goddess called Anoukis with a feathered head-dress and a pet gazelle. One way out of this promiscuity would be to say that these are local traditions going back time out of mind, which it would not be practical to alter, but this is unlikely to have satisfied anyone who thought long and hard about the problem. Monotheism of an unnamed kind would have been a more all-embracing answer. Later classical commentators such as Iamblichus assert directly that Egyptian religion worshipped one supreme god, but these are Neo-Platonist writers, and Neo-Platonists were prone to arguments of this kind. A safer approach is to say that Egyptian religion allowed monotheism, but did not seek to impose it. The innumerable gods and goddesses could be seen as manifestations of an unnamed reality, but they were also valid in their own right.

It is at this point that the revolution of Akhenaten ran into difficulties. The worship of the Aten was exclusive. It is true that Akhenaten made some references to the traditional solar gods, whom he regarded as compatible with the notion of the Aten, but the worship of other gods was at first neglected, and then actively discouraged. It may well be that Akhenaten's chief target was the god Amun, and that it was the worship of this god which he regarded as the 'great lie' which his father and grandfather had listened to but that he declared that he would not. In such a case, other gods could be regarded as mere aberrations which would fade as soon as Amun was toppled from his throne. However, there are occasions when even the plural word 'gods' is hacked out of inscriptions, and it is likely that this too was done on Akhenaten's orders. What the king was doing struck at the root of the tolerance of diversity which the Egyptians not only accepted, but prided themselves in. To Akhenaten, exclusivity was the logical extension of the principle of Ma'at, or truthful harmony, an idea which he adopted as his emblem. To contemporaries this was fanaticism, and fanaticism was not part of Ma'at, who remained a goddess, even if she was an abstract one.

The Restoration Decree of Tutankhamun gives another reason for the hatred that Akhenaten had unleashed. According to this, the economy of the temples was in ruins. This is a political statement, and it is not unknown for politicians to claim that they have inherited a mess from the previous regime. But Egyptian records do not normally make claims of this sort, since to do so would run the risk of inviting divine retribution. The situation in the Restoration Stela may be exaggerated, but the essential truth of what is being said comes through when we consider the role played by the temples in the Egyptian economy. These foundations were not simply ecclesiastical. They could be extensive landowners, and patrons of industries such as linen manufacture and metal working. The larger temples were also major employers of manpower and hirers of labour. In ancient Egypt, unlike medieval Europe, there was no rift between Church and State, although the interests of the two could clash on occasions. Instead, the Egyptian 'Church' was an integral part of the State, and a challenge to the economic health of the one would result in damage to the other. If Akhenaten's opposition to conventional religion led to the closing of temples, as seems certain in the case of Amun and his associates, the disruption of the local community would follow. This inevitably had a domino effect on the national economy, since this depended heavily on the redistribution of local resources. The fact that Akhenaten diverted wealth from traditional temples to the cult of his own god would not have compensated for this; on the contrary, it would have exacerbated things. Egypt after the death of Akhenaten was in trouble, and this would inevitably have been seen as the result of divine wrath. The burden of averting this wrath fell on the shoulders of the young boy who followed Akhenaten and his ephemeral successor on to the throne. This child was originally named Tutankhaten ('Living image of Aten'), and it is increasingly believed that he was the son of Akhenaten by a secondary wife. The exact date of the Restoration Decree is lost, but Tutankhamun, as he had by then become, cannot have been far into his teens when it was written. He was scarcely more than eighteen when he died, after a reign which scraped ten years. We therefore need to ask who really wrote this decree.

Horemheb was a provincial, who originated in the town of Hansu in Middle Egypt. The fact that the town was obscure need not imply that he was too, and it is likely, given his level of education, that he came from the local intelligentsia. Nevertheless, Horemheb seems to have had no links with the aristocracy, and he must have made his way, from routine military and political administration to kingship, on ability rather than patronage. The way that he did this was through the army, and many textbooks describe him as a soldier pure and simple. This is misleading: the early years of Horemheb's career must have been spent under Akhenaten. This ruler was not the complete pacifist he is sometimes made out to be, but, as was the case with Hatshepsut, the role of the army must have been greatly circumscribed under his reign. The reliefs from Akhenaten's capital, Amarna, give the impression that the military's main function during this period was to guard the Pharaoh and provide a backdrop to the festivities which characterised the new cult. Most of Horemheb's activities would have been administrative, whether he was based in the new capital or elsewhere in the country. He knew how to draw up rotas and keep dossiers, and he may well have functioned as the collective memory of his section of the administration. Such a man is not a threat to the regime, since he is thought of as a safe pair of hands. His career would not have been linear, in the modern pattern. He probably went from one commission to another, zigzagging his way rather than moving through a *cursus honorum*. This was not unusual in ancient Egypt, and it had particular advantages in times of trouble. Horemheb may have became adept at remaining as Number Two, especially in any situation where Number One was likely to be targeted.

This aspect of Horemheb explains the way in which he chose to be represented, namely as a scribe. There are statues from the peak of his secular career which show him squatting dutifully, pen and papyrus in hand. Several of his later inscriptions stress his devotion to the god Thoth, and this is most understandable in a scribe, since Thoth was the god of writing, learning and calculation. This is straightforward, but there may have been an additional reason for Horemheb to show his gratitude to this divinity. Thoth was the god of the moon, whose importance in measuring time and the seasons was paramount. However, the moon was also the faithful reflection of the sun. It is quite possible that the

Statue of Horemheb as a scribe. Egyptian sculpture is often stylised, but the features of this portrait are unmistakable, and are likely to be accurate. Now in the Metropolitan Museum of Art, New York.

Egyptians realised through observation that the moon shines by reflected light. Such a discovery would not have been difficult to arrive at, and it would have been compatible with traditional mythology. According to this, the moon, which always keeps its face towards the sun god, was his faithful executor; it derived its being from this association. The sun god of Akhenaten would not have been predisposed to share his light in this way, but the situation after Akhenaten's death was different. The true sun god was once again on earth, but unfortunately he had chosen to incarnate himself in the body of a small child, Tutankhamun. Such a solar being needed someone to reflect his light. An inscription on a stela from the tomb which Horemheb built for himself at Saqqara makes this point clearly. Horemheb is shown in adoration before the sun god, Horakhty, the moon god, Thoth, and the goddess Ma'at, the personification of truth and harmony who had been hijacked by the heretic. The combination of the moon god and justice is standard with Horemheb, and it is close to being a personal religion with him. The great man addresses Thoth as follows:

> Praise to thee, Thoth, lord of Hermopolis, who came into being by his own accord and was not born, unique god, lord of the Netherworld ... who distinguishes the tongues of foreign lands ... mayest thou set the scribe Horemheb firmly by the side of the sovereign, even as thou art at the side of the Lord of the Universe, in the way that thou gavest him [Horemheb] life when he came forth from the womb.

Another text from the same tomb gives in more detail the position which Horemheb attained under the reign of the boy-king:

> Greater than the great, mightier than the mighty ... who follows the king in his journeyings in the southern and the northern land ... chosen by the king above the whole of Egypt to carry out the government of the two shores [of the Nile] ... generalissimo of the lord of the Two Lands ... who was in attendance upon his lord on the battlefield on the day of overcoming the Asiatics.

There are two points here. One is that Horemheb's military career has moved on, since he is now the commander of the Egyptian army, although even here it is likely that his main task was administrative. Interestingly, he took the field in some capacity, presumably in a routine skirmish rather than a major victory, since we hear no more about it. However, the real interest of this text lies elsewhere, since it describes Horemheb as the equivalent of a deputy king. Appointments of this sort may have been made earlier in Egyptian history, since from time to time there would have been a need for them, but this is the first that we can document. Horemheb had become the moon to Tutankhamun's sun,

Head of the goddess Mut, wife of Amun. The features are thought
to represent Mutnodjmet, the consort of Horemheb. Statue now in
the Cairo Museum.

and there is no reason to look further to find the author of the decree which restored the old religion.

The tomb which the regent constructed at Saqqara is now known to be one of the most remarkable in Egypt. It was first unearthed in the early years of the nineteenth century, but no plans of the tomb were made and many of its reliefs were cut from the walls, ending up in collections in the West. However, in the mid-1970s the location was rediscovered by a joint expedition of the Egypt Exploration Society and the Rijksmuseum van Oudheden of Leiden in The Netherlands, whereupon it became possible to document it scientifically. The area in which the tomb was built is one of the most prestigious in the Memphite necropolis, overlooking the flood plain and the site of the capital city, and it also contained the burials of such dignitaries as Maya, the Chancellor of the Exchequer under Tutankhamun. Above ground, Horemheb's complex resembles a middling-sized temple, as befits the deputy to a god, whereas below ground it is a labyrinth, since it was designed as the resting-place of Horemheb and most of his family. One of the shafts was intended for the burial of Horemheb's first wife, whose name is still unknown. Another shaft was the resting-place of his second wife, Mutnodjmet, a lady who is sometimes thought to be related to the Amarna royal family. Forensic evidence suggests that she died in childbirth. When completed, this monument would have been the finest private tomb in Egypt, and in its restored state it is one of the sights of Saqqara.

Tutankhamun's death has not been explained, and it is not known whether it was expected, but the fact that the young king died without an heir produced a crisis. His widow took the most unusual step of writing to the king of the Hittites, asking for one of his sons in marriage, since she had no intention of marrying any of her husband's advisers. The Hittite prince died in mysterious circumstances on his way to Egypt, an incident which pushed both powers to the brink of war. Horemheb, as chief of the army, must have been involved in these events, but the surprising thing is that he does not become Tutankhamun's successor. Instead, this role devolves upon the High Priest of Amun, Ay, a survivor of the Amarna period who was probably a brother of Akhenaten's mother. Ay's links with the royal family may have been a factor in this, but Horemheb presumably had the backing of the army. The fact that Horemheb did not press home this advantage raises a suspicion that the pair had made a deal. Ay was the older of the two candidates, and he had the backing of the priesthood of Amun. He could be ousted, but this would amount to civil war on top of a military stand-off with the Hittites. The easier option would be to let him serve out his time in return for a guarantee that Horemheb would succeed him. The chances of survival in ancient Egypt were somewhat different from those of the modern world, but the odds were still on Horemheb's side. Perhaps he had come to value the position of deputy, and was content to let Ay pick up what could prove to be a poisoned chalice. As it was, Ay's reign lasted four years.

We have seen Horemheb's tendency to clothe political events in the trappings of mythology, and this may have been a genuine feature of his personality. The decrees which he issued as king have a realistic tone to them, and it is clear that he had few illusions about human nature. However, this need not mean that his piety was hypocritical, since he would have felt that the gods, who had been slighted by Akhenaten, were guiding him to make the necessary restitution. Members of the armed forces risk their lives, and they have a tendency not to turn their backs on religion, whether ancient or modern. As has been said, there are no atheists in a landing craft. Horemheb was no theologian, but he would have sensed that practical politics and divine will went hand-in-hand, and this was what the times needed.

The Coronation Text of Horemheb is mainly known from a statue showing the king, together with his queen, Mutnodjmet, which is now in the Museo Egizio in Turin. The text is written on the back of the couple's throne. In this long inscription, Horemheb is represented as the protégé of the god of his home town, Horus of Hansu. This god had singled him out for kingship before he was born (one may suspect retrospective wishful thinking here), and placed him under his special protection. In due course Horemheb became 'chief spokesman' of the Two Lands, which can only be another way of referring to his regency. On one occasion, he says that he was called in to calm down the Palace when it had fallen into a rage. Some have taken this as a reference to Akhenaten, whose personality may well have been unstable, but the fact that this took place when Horemheb was regent argues for the reign of Tutankhamun. In this case we are dealing either with a boyish tantrum, or a plot by rival advisers to discredit Horemheb. If this episode happened in the reign of Ay, it would signify a temporary hitch in the pact between the two men. At this point in the text Horemheb is under the protection, not of his local god, but of Thoth, the moon-scribe who was his principal patron. These gods effectively take the place of earthly parents, and it is interesting that Horemheb never names his mother or father.

When time was come for Horemheb to come into his so-called inheritance, the text describes how Horus of Hansu set off along the Nile to the temples of Luxor and Karnak, where he introduced his adopted son as the rightful lord of Egypt. Amun, the god of Thebes, saw immediately that this was right, and crowned him there and then (c. 1323 BC). This is an unusual way for a king of Egypt to begin his reign, but the alliance between the gods Horus and Amun can easily be seen as the mythological expression of the deal which had been made between Horemheb and Ay, the former Priest of Amun.

After the coronation in Thebes, Horemheb sets off north, where he renovates the temples of the gods, which had been found 'wrecked, from an earlier time'. He restores the gods' images, replenishes their temples, and fills them with priests and acolytes, taken from the army. The last point is important, since it shows the king turning to his natural power-base. The army had been loyal to him for twenty years or more, and it was time for their reward. This part of the Coronation Text duplicates the events of the Restoration Decree of Tutankhamun, but, since the latter was essentially Horemheb's work, the anachronism is understandable. Horemheb was the real restorer of the old religion, and gods and people were going to know it.

More clues to the nature of Horemheb's reign are contained in a judicial edict found in front of the Ninth Pylon of the temple of Karnak. This text is one of the most comprehensive treatments of social reform to survive from ancient Egypt. Essentially, the new king runs through a list of abuses which are prevalent in the land, denounces them, and lays down punishments, many of them severe. Most scholars have taken this text as a comment on the state of Egypt after the death of Akhenaten, but Horemheb never mentions this, even though there would have been political capital to be made from doing so. One of the abuses, the requisitioning of supplies from local mayors by royal officials under false pretences, is stated to go back to Tuthmosis III, the successor of Hatshepsut. What is likely is that the edict is a blanket treatment of problems, some of long standing, while others may have been exacerbated by the economic instability caused by the Amarna period. Whatever the history, the text represents Horemheb as true to his scribal type, reaching for pen and papyrus-scroll, and writing down his remedies for good government. It is significant that the first abuse which he tackles is one which is ascribed to the army; Horemheb clearly had the confidence, and the power, to take on injustice wherever it arose, even among his own supporters. Members of the armed forces who wrongly confiscated boats used on government service were to be punished with amputation of the nose and exile to the region of Sile, on the frontier with

Sinai. This sounds an adequate deterrent, although it may have been lenient compared with the alternatives available.

Soldiers had got into the habit of entering private houses and commandeering hides, which suggests that there had been a shortage of leather in parts of the country. Leather was essential for body armour and for certain weapons, but the punishment for a soldier caught stealing it was fixed at one hundred blows and five open wounds. It is to be hoped, for the soldiers' sake, that the number of animals in the country was on the increase. Conversely, certain taxes were remitted, such as the one levied on the law courts for silver and gold, since exacting these taxes had led to malpractice. The cost of this remission must have fallen on the Crown, and the extent to which Horemheb was prepared to enforce justice becomes clear. State employees were to be rewarded more handsomely than before, particularly at the public occasions when Pharaoh mingled with his household; here too the king is prepared to put his money where his mouth is, since he knows that underpaid and discontented civil servants are a source of corruption. The tone of the Edict's clauses can be gauged from the following extract dealing with cases of extortion:

> As for those monkey-handlers who go around levying taxes in the South and North, extorting grain from the citizenry by use of an *oipe*-measure of 50 *hin* and so short-changing them ... while others go in the opposite direction, exacting an *oipe* from private individuals as of right ... My Majesty orders these to be suppressed entirely, to prevent them wronging persons by such fraud.

A *hin* is a measure of approximately half a litre, and the true exchange-rate was forty to the *oipe* rather than fifty. The mark-up is not inconsiderable. The term 'monkey-handler' is not to be taken literally, but is probably the late Eighteenth-Dynasty equivalent of 'shyster'. It goes without saying that the real handlers of monkeys can have done nothing to merit such an unjust reputation. There are other colourful expressions in this text, which Horemheb may well have picked up during his army career. The Edict of Horemheb is an impressive piece of legislation, not least because it is rooted in a knowledge of human nature.

Horemheb seems to have been childless; at least no son of his survived into adulthood. The solution which he found for this is typically shrewd. He turned to a lieutenant of his named Pramesse ('The sun god is the one who bore him'). This man originated in the Delta, and was thus untainted by the aristocracies of Memphis and Thebes, not to mention Amarna. Before long the lieutenant became *vizier*, the equivalent of a prime minister in a political monarchy, and finally he was made deputy to the king, exactly as Horemheb himself had been under Tutankhamun. The arrangement worked equally well, and in due course Pramesse dropped the vulgar definite article at the beginning of his name, succeeding his master as Ramesses I. Later historians took this event as the beginning of the next dynasty, since the royal name Ramesses became so common in the following generations that it made sense to start the era with the one who began the habit, but contemporaries considered that Horemheb was the true founder of the dynasty, and a posthumous cult grew up around him in this capacity. This is clear from the finds at the Memphite tomb of Horemheb, which became a focal point for members of the Ramesside clan. The tomb was kept for members of Horemheb's own family, and the scenes on the walls were modified by the addition of the royal cobra, the *uraeus*, to the forehead of the owner. It may be that Horemheb would have wished to be buried there himself, but tradition and theology were against this. Instead, he went ahead with a tomb in the Valley of the Kings, richly decorated, but monotonous as only kings' tombs can be in ancient Egypt, with gods processing along the walls and endlessly welcoming their new colleague into the afterlife. Perhaps the Number Two slot had its compensations after all.

The scarcity of year-dates from the reign of Horemheb is a problem. The highest known for certain is a year 13, which occurs on a jar from the Memphite tomb. An inscription of year 16 has been published, mentioning an otherwise unknown campaign far into Syria, but this inscription is believed to be a forgery. The figure of sixteen years is plausible, given the likely age of Horemheb at his accession, but the question is complicated by a later text from the reign of Ramesses II, which is known as the Inscription of Mose. This is an account of a legal case concerning the ownership of a plot of land, a dispute which had dragged on for generations. At one point, the narrator refers to events which happened before his time, and which he ascribes to year 59 of Horemheb. It is most unlikely that Horemheb ever reached such an advanced score, and historians are agreed that this is an artificial number which incorporates the years of Akhenaten and his ephemeral successors into the reign of the general who replaced them. This was a useful way of erasing all trace of Atenism from the record, and also of crediting the man who was thought to be the founder of the new era with a more impressive period of office. If this is the explanation, the Mose reference implies that the true reign of Horemheb lasted at least twenty-seven years. A mention of a year 27 is found in a graffito from the king's own mortuary temple, but this may be a record from a later reign, and thus irrelevant. At the moment, we simply do not know how long Horus of Hansu and Thoth of Hermopolis permitted Horemheb to rule over Egypt. This problem has implications for the chronology of the period which preceded him, but it is of lesser importance when it comes to considering the soldier-king's role in Egyptian history.

Some historians of this period have raised the question whether Horemheb was a reformer or a reactionary. This question is not straightforward. One way to deal with it is to evade it, by denying that the distinction is a valid one, but this too brings problems. Horemheb lived in the aftermath of a drastic reform, that of Akhenaten. This reform had gone wrong, and the remedy lay in reversing what had taken place. In this sense, Horemheb is reactionary, but this need not mean that he turned his back on the impulse to make things function more justly. He may have seen himself as restoring a primeval state of well-being, which had been subverted by fanaticism, but his knowledge of human weakness would have warned him that turning the clock back to an imagined age of innocence was not the full answer. In modern terms, he can be placed at the progressive end of the conservative tendency, which is something of a paradox, although the centre-right can be an effective standpoint if one wants to get things done. Horemheb's own estimate of himself is contained in the epilogue to his Edict, where he says:

> As long as my life on earth remains, it shall be spent making monuments for the gods. I shall be renewed unceasingly, like the moon ... one whose limbs shed light on the ends of the earth like the disc of the sun god.

By 'monuments' the Egyptians understood works of justice and piety as well as buildings made of stone, and reform would have been equally pleasing to the gods. The simile involving the moon may seem bizarre to the modern mind, but it was not to Horemheb. It is a reference to the god Thoth, who had guided his life, and it is a reminder of the position he held under a series of sun kings. It also recalls a passage in the *Wisdom of Amenemope*, an ethical and philosophical text which is not far removed in date from Horemheb. In this text the moon is the eye of justice, whose face gazes at the wrongdoer even in the darkness where he tries to hide. That is how Horemheb chose to be remembered.

CHAPTER FIVE

The First Egyptologist

Khaemwise, c. 1285–1225 BC

Ramesses II is the most famous of the Pharaohs, and there is no doubt that he intended this to be so. He is the Jupiter of the Pharaonic system, and this simile is appropriate, since the giant planet is brilliant at a distance but is essentially a ball of gas. Ramesses II, whose throne-name eventually gave rise to the Ozymandias of Strabo and Shelley, is the hieroglyphic equivalent of hot air. His name nowadays is known to every donkey-boy and tourist tout in the Nile valley, which is as it should be. Nevertheless, the truth is that Ramesses has gained the afterlife he would have wished: his mummy flies to Paris to be exhibited and re-autopsied, and a series of airport-lounge bestsellers by a French author tells the story of his life to millions of readers. Yul Brynner captured the essence of his personality in the film *The Ten Commandments*, and he is often thought of as the Pharaoh of the Exodus. The history behind this has been much debated, but there is little doubt that the character of Ramesses fits the picture of the arrogant ruler who rejects divine demands. His battle against the Hittites at Qadesh in Syria was a near defeat, caused by an elementary failure of military intelligence, and saved only by the last-minute arrival of reinforcements from the Lebanese coast. In Ramesses' account, which figures large on many of his monuments, this near-debacle turns into the mother of all victories. James Baikie (1866–1931), a Scottish divine with a pawky streak, who wrote an excellent guidebook to the monuments of Egypt without feeling the need ever to visit the place, described the battle thus: 'The Egyptian court, we imagine, must have been slightly weary of the whole business. Ramesses, however, was not weary of seeing and hearing of his prowess, and it was Ramesses who called the tune, though the unfortunate soldiers of Amun and Re had paid the piper.' [1]

The traditional capitals, Memphis and Thebes, are not good enough for this Pharaoh, and he plans a new one in the Delta, modestly named Piramesse, which can be rendered as Ramessopolis. Not even Akhenaten had dared to name his city after himself. It must be admitted that the man thinks large, and this extends to his family, since he assures us that he is the father of more than 100 sons. With daughters he was not so successful, since he only mentions sixty of these, but it is possible that he had ceased to count them. Previous Pharaohs had adhered to the rule that, in temple design, incised relief was used on the exterior walls, since it casts strong shadows. Inside the temples, however, bas-relief was employed, since it does not produce such contrasts and creates a sensuous effect in the semi-dark. Unfortunately, bas-relief takes time, since the background needs to be cut away from around the figures. From now on, Ramesses decides to double the standard rate of temple-building, by seeing to it that most of the work is done in instant, inexpensive, incised relief. Akhenaten had tried the same trick, but he was in a genuine hurry, since he had abandoned traditional cities and needed a new one for his god. Ramesses II does not have this excuse. He is, when all is said, on the side of the cheap and nasty.

Revisionist accounts of Ramesses' reign make several points in his favour. The battle of Qadesh was followed by the international peace treaty with the Hittites, a copy of which is on the wall of the General Assembly building of the United Nations. This is surely an achievement. A more general point is that modesty, as we have seen in the case of Hatshepsut, was not thought to be a Pharaonic virtue, and Ramesses is merely the logical extension of this. If kings of Egypt are great by definition, there is nothing wrong in going out of one's way to be the greatest; it is to be the essence of the thing. Another mitigating factor is the origin of Ramesses' family. The prototype of Ozymandias was the grandson of Ramesses I, a respected figure but known mainly as the man in the equivalent of the grey suit next to Horemheb. If Ramesses II took a look at recent history, he would have seen the anarchy of the Amarna period, an episode which was being rapidly purged from the record. Beyond this, however, lay the family of the Tuthmosides, a dynasty which was associated with prosperity, elegance, the growth of empire, and success. Another figure which loomed over the king was his father, Seti I, whose reign was one of the high points of Egyptian art, since it is marked by balance and restraint. These were the hard acts which it was Ramesses' duty to follow, and one way of doing this would be to bypass Seti, and to upstage the Tuthmosides by shouting louder than they had, so that they would no longer be heard. Ramesses II was temperamentally suited to this kind of role, and the gods gave him a reign of sixty-seven years in which to perfect it.

It is a relief to turn from this vainglorious man to his family, complicated though this was. Minor wives proliferated throughout the reign, but there are only two principal queens. One of these, Nefertari, is well known, thanks to her exquisitely decorated tomb in the Valley of the Queens at Luxor. This has been restored, and is one of the sights of Egypt. Good art is not unknown in Ramesses' reign, especially in the earlier years when artists from his father's court were still active, and it continued to flourish when not subjected to the dead weight of the king's ego. The monuments of Nefertari cluster in the south of the country, and

Nefertari, wife of Ramesses II, is escorted into the afterlife by the goddess Isis. From her tomb in the Valley of the Queens, Luxor.

this may in some way have been her sphere of influence. She owed her place in the king's affections partly to her charm, to which her inscriptions often refer, but also to the fact that she was the mother of several princes and princesses, including the eldest son and heir, who was given the cumbersome name Amenhiwenim-mef, 'Amun is on his right hand'. Nefertari, whose name means 'The loveliest of them all', seems to have died before the thirtieth year of the reign. The second principal wife is Isinofre ('Isis the beautiful'), who is less well known. The influence of this queen is more detectable in the north of the country, although her tomb seems also to have been in Luxor. She was more or less a contemporary of her rival, and she could boast that she had borne the king his second son, ingeniously named Ramesses, and a favourite daughter, who was given the Canaanite name Bintanath, 'Daughter of (the Syrian goddess) Anath'. Isinofre was also the mother of the fourth in line to the throne, a prince named Khaemwise, and it is to this unusual character that we turn.

We have no way of knowing whether Khaemwise took after his mother, but we can safely say that he did not take after his father. Khaemwise's name means 'Manifest in Thebes', but names can be misleading. Most of his inscriptions and monuments are found in or near Memphis, and it may be that he saw this city as his home. This would be in line with the theory that his mother was also based in the north of the country. Alternatively, he may have been drawn to the place because of its antiquity, and because of the wealth of monuments that it contained even in his day. The past fascinated Khaemwise, and as a result Khaemwise fascinates Egyptologists, who see him as one of their own, although so far there is no popular work devoted to him. The truth is complex, but the title can stand. To us, he is the first Egyptologist, and, although there is no ancient Egyptian word for Egyptologist, it is a concept that this scholarly prince would have recognised.

Khaemwise was not entirely alone. The Ramesside period shows an increased interest in what we may term personal piety, and a sense of history. The upheavals of the Amarna period, and the reflections on the nature of Egyptian culture which followed it, would have encouraged this tendency, if they did not create it. Natural curiosity is shown by a hieroglyphic inscription on a fossilised sea-urchin, which was found by a Ramesside scribe in the desert near Heliopolis, where he dedicated it to the gods, because it was a wonder. Visits to ancient monuments became fashionable, and in the opening chapter of this book we met the scribe Nashuyu, who went to see the monuments of Djoser and Teti at Saqqara, and left a graffito about it. Other such records are known from this period. However, this remained something of a leisure-time activity. With Khaemwise, the occasional afternoon outing becomes a full-time occupation.

Most of the principal sons of Ramesses are shown from time to time on his interminable battle reliefs, and for a while this is true of Khaemwise. He may even have seen military action early in his life, but it was soon clear that his talents were not going to lie in this direction. The prince gravitated towards the priesthood of Ptah, the principal god of Memphis. One of the names for the sanctuary of this god was Hikuptah, 'the house of the spirit [ka] of Ptah', an expression which passed to Ugarit on the Syrian coast, where it developed into one of the names for the country as a whole. This was later picked up by Greek traders, in the form Aigyptos, whence the modern equivalent. Ptah was a patron of craftsmanship and technology, and there was a rarefied side to his theology. Khaemwise may have learnt as an apprentice how Ptah created the universe using his heart (or mind), which conceptualised the elements of creation, and his tongue, which articulated and named them. This concept has similarities to the Judaic notion of the Word of God, which in turn influenced the Christian doctrine of the Logos; certainly it is a remarkable feat of abstraction. Such things are characteristic of a civilisation which created divine kingship, derived a unified principal from the plethora of local gods and goddesses, and put together the only rational calendar ever devised, which they liberated from the incompatibility between the length of the solar year and the mathematics of the lunar month. Other calendars, including our own, are a mess in comparison.

Khaemwise informs us that he entered the service of the god Ptah while still a youth. He no doubt rose through the ranks,

An idealised portrait of Prince Khaemwise, showing him with the conventional lock of youthful hair which was an emblem of the setem-priest. Relief from one of the prince's monuments at Saqqara.

although his rise will not have been hindered by the fact that he was related to the living god who ruled the realm. The priesthood has been an outlet for spare princes and sons of the aristocracy in many cultures, but with Khaemwise one has the impression that he was the right man in the right place. His ecclesiastical career reached its peak when he was appointed High Priest of Ptah at Memphis. This appointment may have taken place in the year 25, when Khaemwise would have been about thirty. In traditional terms he was the head of the religious hierarchy, although during the New Kingdom the post of First Prophet of Amun at Karnak was more influential. One of the duties of the High Priest of Memphis was to help crown the Pharaoh, and he was in effect the keeper of much of the royal protocol. Even Alexander the Great, when he arrived in Egypt, is said to have submitted to some sort of coronation ceremony in Memphis. In addition to his duties towards the living king, the High Priest also acted in a filial role at the royal burial, and he is often shown wearing a leopard-skin, a traditional sign of prestigious rank, and with a lock of hair dangling from his forehead, which is a symbol of youth. A High Priest of Ptah could be shown like this even when he was well into his seventies; as often in Egyptian art, it is the icon which takes precedence over the mundane reality. A title given to the High Priest in this capacity was the Setem, a word of great antiquity and uncertain meaning, and it is under this alternative name that Khaemwise frequently appears. In reality he received this title some years before he became High Priest, which had the effect of marking him out as the heir presumptive to the office.

The High Priest of Memphis had access to the second finest temple library in Egypt, and he may have had the right to use the finest, which was at Heliopolis, a shortish journey to the north-east of Memphis. Antiquarian research came naturally to Khaemwise, and some of his inscriptions make the point that he was never happier than when reading the records of earlier times. His compositions are full of obscure words and convoluted turns of phrase. In this respect, he can settle into the familiar role of the armchair professor or scholarly priest. This is what he would be in the modern world, but it is more important to see how he fits into his own society.

Ramesses II's attitude to his sons must have been ambiguous. He could be as proud of them as any father, trumpeting about them constantly on his monuments, but they were also a source of rivalry. Many of the princes predeceased him, which is partly explicable by the great age to which he survived, but it is not entirely explicable in this way. Some of the sons may have been perceived as threatening, in which case they would have been sidelined in one way or another. A policy of divide and rule by the king would have led to rivalries, some of which may have been deadly. Khaemwise's scholarly activities were not a threat, although there may have been times when he needed to hide his knowledge, since contradicting or correcting Ramesses II might not have been a good career move. The son had the intelligence to realise that he could use his antiquarian interests in a way which reflected glory on his overwhelming parent. It is no accident that the reign of this ruler has given us a number of king-lists, either on papyrus (a fragmentary one exists in Turin, which would have been invaluable had it been preserved intact), or written on the walls of temples and even private tombs. One was found in the temple which Ramesses II built to the god Osiris at Abydos. In this composition, the dead kings of the past are assimilated, not simply to Osiris as is usual, but to the figure of Ramesses himself. He is their embodiment, and therefore the culmination of the entire historical process. To commemorate the kings of the past, and to find out more about them, was to commemorate the king *par excellence* who enshrined them. Archaeology has always been a promiscuous discipline, hiring out its favours to political ideas, notions of ethnicity, or religious beliefs, depending on the needs of the client. The past was going to serve the present, and Khaemwise was willing to be part of this.

At some point Khaemwise must have set out to walk the plateau of Giza and Saqqara, inspecting the pyramids of the Old Kingdom which had looked out over Memphis for more than a millennium. Even in his day some of these were past their best, partly through the effects of time, but also owing to the Pharaohs' habit of recycling the monuments of their predecessors whenever they had the opportunity. A programme of restoration was set in progress, which could serve a variety of purposes: the memory of the great monarchs of old would be honoured, knowledge of the past could be enriched, and the monuments themselves would be spiritually updated, so that they became part of the glory which was Ramesses. Instead of a pyramid, the late Fourth-Dynasty king Shepseskaf built himself an unusual oblong tomb, of the type known as a *mastaba*. It was already 1,200 years old when Khaemwise inspected it, but this too came in for the treatment. The names of Shepseskaf were inscribed on its exterior wall, facing those of Ramesses, and below this was set the following:

> His Majesty instructed the High Priest of Ptah and Setem, Khaemwise, to inscribe the cartouche of king Shepseskaf, since his name could not be found on the face of his pyramid [sic], inasmuch as the Setem Khaemwise loved to restore the monuments of the kings, making firm again what had fallen into ruin.

This is piety indeed, and the Egyptian words which can be translated as 'pious' and 'piety' are constantly used by Khaemwise. 'Consider these pious works' is one of his refrains. However, the piety was also a form of flattery. An important part of the king's religious function was to dispel darkness and chaos from the land, and rescuing monuments from oblivion was as good a way as any of demonstrating this. Variations of this text appear on several monuments at Saqqara and nearby, and there must have been others, now lost. However, a more intimate sign of Khaemwise's love of the past is found in a fragmentary text on the statue of a man named Kawab. Khaemwise must have come across this statue somewhere near the tomb of this man, a son of the builder of the Great Pyramid, who had lived and died more than 1,000 years before him. In effect, Khaemwise was conducting an excavation at Giza. His reaction to this find he describes himself:

It was the High Priest and Prince Khaemwise who delighted in this statue of the king's son Kawab, which he discovered in the fill of a shaft [?] in the area of the well of his father Khufu. [He acted] so as to place it in the favour of the gods, among the glorious spirits of the chapel of the necropolis, because he loved the noble ones who dwelt in antiquity before him, and the excellence of everything they made, in very truth, a million times.

There is no better description of what it is to be an Egyptologist. The reference to the chapel in which this statue was rededicated suggests that it functioned as a sort of museum for objects rescued from the sands, and this idea is not fanciful, because other examples of royal collections of antiquities are known from our sources. The reference to the nobility of the past may not be mere romance; Khaemwise could have found some aspects of the world he lived in unsatisfactory, and not always noble.

Khaemwise's reading extended to matters of theology, and he began to think about the implications of one of the most characteristic aspects of Egyptian religion, the cult of sacred animals. One of these, the Apis bull, we have already mentioned, but it is time to return to it, since it was destined to play a part in Khaemwise's life. The Apis was based in Memphis, where it had its own temple complete with stall, and it occupied the place in the animal world which Pharaoh did in the human. One of its titles was 'king of every sacred animal'. Another of its epithets was 'incarnation of Ptah', where the first word comes from a root meaning 'to repeat'. Translation is difficult, but to use a term derived from Hinduism, we can say that the Apis was an avatar, and he represented the god of Memphis whose priest Khaemwise was. The Apis, like a Pharaoh, eventually grew old and died, whereupon he went to Osiris. The burial places of the earlier Apis bulls are unknown, but from the reign of Amenophis III they began to be interred in the desert at Saqqara, to the west of the Step Pyramid. As it happens,

The avenue leading to Khaemwise's Serapeum. Nineteenth-century drawing made at the time of the excavation by Auguste Mariette. It was on this avenue that Hor of Sebennytos dreamt he met the ghost, as related in Chapter 8 (p. 151).

this innovation is associated with another king's son, Tuthmosis, who was the elder brother of Akhenaten. This prince, who would have come to the throne as Tuthmosis V if he had lived, took an interest in animal-cults: in the Cairo Museum there is a sarcophagus which he caused to be made for his pet feline, which shows the animal in the form of a mummy, bearing the somewhat hybrid name 'Osiris the she-cat'. Khaemwise felt an affinity with this unusual prince, and may have modelled himself upon him. If Tuthmosis had lived, there would not have been an Amarna period, and cults like the Apis could be seen almost as an antidote to Akhenaten and his experiments in heresy. There was more that could be done for the Apis, and Khaemwise set about doing it.

The last Apis to be buried in isolation at Saqqara was laid to rest in year 30 of Ramesses II. The next step was the excavation of an entire catacomb below the area of the isolated Apis burials. Here the bulls were to be accommodated in a series of vaults, each containing a granite sarcophagus, weighing up to eighty tons. The vaults were linked by a communicating corridor, excavated by Khaemwise's masons, and running through the rock for a distance of more than 100 yards. This gallery fulfilled its purpose down to the beginning of the Twenty-sixth Dynasty, when the whole was enlarged. The later galleries in the complex were still in use in the time of Cleopatra, and they are familiar to modern tourists as the Serapeum. Above the catacomb there was a temple dedicated to Osiris-Apis, the collective aspect of the dead Apises who had lived on earth, as well as to the living Apis. In his dedicatory inscription, Khaemwise allows himself a touch of bombast which was standard in inscriptions of this sort:

> O Setem-priests and High Priests of the house of Ptah, divine fathers, and duty-priests ... who are before the god, who shall enter this temple which I have made for the living Apis and who shall look upon these things which I have done, engraved upon its stone walls ... Surely this will seem a pious thing to you, when you compare the ancestors, with their poor and ignorant work ... Remember my name in [your] decrees ...

This sniping at the ancestors sounds like a lapse of taste when compared with Khaemwise's other inscriptions, but the superlatives are justified in such a case, and the gods were used to rhetoric of this sort. He was a High Priest, after all, and a son of the master of hyperbole. It is also likely that such an inscription needed to be run past Khaemwise's father.

If Khaemwise was the first Egyptologist, he was also the first to realise that to study Egyptology it helps if one has an income. The priesthood of Ptah was no doubt rewarding, financially as well as intellectually, and he would also have received some settlement as a son of Ramesses. He built up a considerable estate, which may well have functioned on its own, leaving him free to study his archaic texts.

In Leiden, there is a papyrus which contains part of the logbook of one of his ships. The text covers a few days in the winter of year 52 of the king's reign (c. 1228 BC). At the beginning of the voyage, the ship is moored at Piramesse, the new capital in the Delta. Deliveries to the crew are listed, and comings and goings recorded, with messengers from time to time leaving for Memphis with letters for the Setem, as Khaemwise is regularly termed in this document. In addition to members of the crew, there are other persons who appear to be passengers. Then the ship sets sail, and on the third day of the third month of winter, 'the sky filled with a strong south wind'. This is characteristic of the period from February to April in Egypt, and it can presage sandstorms. The following day, in the evening, the boat docked at Heliopolis. Such a journey was not for pleasure, nor for the purpose simply of moving passengers from one place to another. It was a trading enterprise, with produce brought on board and sold again further along the river. Such a boat could easily have paid for itself over a few years. In addition, there is evidence that Khaemwise's trading activities could stretch wider than this. In the somewhat fantastical tale known as *The Voyage of Wenamun*, the eponymous hero has a long debate with Zekerba'al, the ruler of Byblos on the Phoenician coast. At one point, the wily Levantine remonstrates with him:

'See now, I have not done to you what was done to the messengers of Khaemwise. They spent seventeen years in this land, and they died on the spot.' Then he told his cupbearer, 'Take him to see the tomb where they lie.' But I said to him, 'Do not make me see it.'

The messengers of this tale would have gone to Lebanon for

the same reason that Wenamun did: to buy cedar wood and other timber, either for one of the temples or directly for the Crown. There are some elements in *Wenamun* which are reminiscent of Homer's *Odyssey*, but this is not a reason to doubt that such a mission could have taken place. The text is later than Khaemwise by about two centuries, but there may well be fact in it as well as fiction.

So far we have created a picture of a tranquil scholar with considerable means, and this would have been true for much of Khaemwise's career. However, as the reign wore on the demands that were made on the king's fourth son continued to grow. One by one his elder brothers passed away, and Khaemwise came closer to the throne. This in itself would have meant greater protocol, and with it other responsibilities. However, the exacerbating factor was Ramesses' addiction to publicity. Pharaohs who reigned for thirty years were entitled to celebrate a jubilee. Thereafter they were permitted more jubilees, but at discreet intervals. Ramesses became a jubilee junkie, celebrating these jamborees in years 30, 33, 36, 39, 40, 42, 45, 48, 52, 54, 57, 60, 63 and 66. The burden of organising many of these fell upon Khaemwise, and he will have spent months on each occasion travelling up and down the country, seeing that the right statues of the right gods were available for the festivities, embracing local dignitaries, and generally drawing up plans for the ceremonials. This was good for his standing at court, but there must have been occasions when he longed for the quiet and cool of his temple libraries, and there may have been times when he silently wished for the process to come to its natural end.

Instead of his father, it was Khaemwise who came to an end. The endless procession of durbars wore him out, and, by regnal year 60, the heir apparent was no longer Khaemwise, but the king's thirteenth son, an elderly prince named Merneptah who was to succeed to the throne. So Khaemwise's gods willed.

One of the most remarkable discoveries of recent years has been made near the entrance to the Valley of the Kings. This is the tomb numbered KV5. Strictly speaking, this tomb was already known, since it had been glanced at in 1825 by an adventurer named James Burton. It was assumed to be incomplete, perhaps a false start for the tomb of Ramesses II which was built further inside the Valley. However, an American team returned to this tomb in the 1990s, cleared it out, and concluded that it was nothing less than the communal resting-place of Ramesses' many sons. It was constructed on two levels within the rock, and the whole bears a resemblance to a multi-storey car park. Its various chambers may amount to 150, which would almost correspond to the round numbers of sons and daughters which Ramesses boasted. Work on this remarkable monument will take years, but it is not difficult to see similarities between this catacomb for human royalty and the Serapeum, a complex which was intended for the royalty of the animal world. It is possible that Khaemwise had a hand in both projects, but, whatever the original intention, the High Priest of Memphis was not destined to be buried in KV5.

We are not sure precisely where Khaemwise is buried. In the early 1850s the French archaeologist Auguste Mariette began clearing the Serapeum, making an unbroken series of major discoveries, but working in considerable haste. In the centre of the main gallery built by Khaemwise Mariette claimed to have found the mummified remains of a man wearing a golden funerary mask, accompanied by jewellery bearing the cartouches of Ramesses II. However, the mummy has now disappeared, and there is even doubt whether it was human, whilst the fact that Mariette was resorting to explosives at this stage of his work adds a vigorous but somewhat imprecise note to the record. Khaemwise could have been buried in the Serapeum, or somewhere near it, and it may be that he is like Imhotep, still waiting for excavators beneath the sands of Saqqara.

A twist to the tale is added by a Japanese team, who in the 1990s started to excavate a building on the top of a natural rise looking out over the area of the Serapeum. This rise was clearly visible from the excavations in the Sacred Animal Necropolis which were mentioned in Chapter 1, and the author, who in the late 1960s was a junior member of the excavation team, remembers wondering what lay on top of this prominent hill. At the time, this area was a military zone, and out of bounds to archaeologists. The building found by the Japanese turned out to be a curious temple-like structure, decorated with texts and reliefs in honour of Khaemwise. Its design is unique in Egyptian architecture, and it is probably the result of Khaemwise's researches into arcane literature. It is a shrine to the dead prince's cult, but as yet there is no sign of his tomb. From the temple on the ridge, the spirit of Khaemwise could have gazed west, to the endless desert, or taken in the view of all the pyramids from Giza in the north to Dahshur in the south, while to the east he could have looked towards Memphis, his earthly home.

Khaemwise has the most colourful afterlife of any character in this volume. In order to do this he had to give up his personal name, while his administrative title, the Setem, was garbled into Setne. It is under this name that he appears in a number of tales written in demotic, a form of hieroglyphic shorthand, some 1,000 years after his death. The Setne of these tales is sometimes recognisable as the scholarly priest who spent his time reading the writings on the monuments, but he has picked up some ribald characteristics over the intervening years. The first tale, which is Ptolemaic, is now in the Cairo Museum. Here we find Setne in characteristic style, reading hieroglyphs on temple walls, when he receives a tip-off that a book containing the secrets of the universe is hidden in an ancient tomb. Eventually he finds the tomb and enters it, where he is entertained by a friendly family of ghosts who tell him their life story. He rewards the ghosts' hospitality by making off with the book, and the text describes how he came back along the tomb shaft with the light from the magical scroll illuminating his path. The ghosts seek revenge by visiting a series of humiliations on Setne, designed to bring him to his senses. The climax comes when the ghosts create a phantom woman of outstanding beauty, named Tabubu. Setne sees this lady one day in the temple of Ptah, and tries to arrange an assignation with her. Her reply can be paraphrased as, 'What sort of woman do you think I am? Here's my address.' Setne proceeds with his assignation, but the phantom woman, after making a series of crippling financial demands, disappears into thin air at the crucial moment, leaving Setne lying on the ground in a state of undisguised embarrassment. At this moment Pharaoh walks in. As the text puts it, 'Setne tried to rise, but he could not rise because of the shame that he was in, for he had no clothes on.' This inappropriate event convinces him that struggle against the ghosts is futile. He makes his peace with them, and they are once more laid to rest, with their book.

Setne learnt something as a result of this encounter, and he learns something else in the second tale, which dates from the beginning of the Roman period and is in the British Museum. In this story, Setne and his wife have no son, but following a dream a miraculous child is born to them. The child, Si-Osiri ('Son of Osiris'), turns out to be something of a portentous know-all. One day father and son see two funerals, one of a rich man and another of a poor man with no one to mourn him. Setne expresses the wish that, when he dies, he may be buried in splendour like the rich man, but Si-Osiri replies that, if his father knew anything at all, he would pray to be buried like the poor one. Si-Osiri takes Setne to the necropolis, where they find a tomb-entrance which leads directly to the Underworld. There, in one part of eternity, are the damned, suffering great torments, including being made to plait ropes which everlasting donkeys immediately chew to ribbons. One man has the pivot of the door of the netherworld fixed in his eye; he is the rich man whose funeral they had seen, and whose conduct in life has been found wanting by the judges of eternity. Finally they come into the presence of Osiris, who is attended by a man in radiant robes, taking the god's dictation. He is the poor man, whose life had been found good. The similarity to the parable of Dives and Lazarus has often been noted, although the idea that paradise consists of becoming a bureaucrat is typically Egyptian. After all this it emerges that Si-Osiri is a famous magician from the past who has arranged to be reborn in order to save Egypt from disaster at the hands of a Nubian sorcerer. His work accomplished, he vanishes, phoenix-like, in flames, and that night Setne's wife conceives a real son.

It is impossible to know how much of the character of the historical Khaemwise is preserved in the Setne stories, which were highly popular in later Egypt. The odds are that Khaemwise would have been ashamed of Setne and his unacademic adventures, but this is not a problem for us. We can be content that both characters are part of the richness of Egyptian civilisation.

CHAPTER SIX

The Temple Scribe's Petition

Petiese, c. 583–511 BC

In 525 BC Egypt became part of the Persian empire. The country had seen foreign domination before this time, and not all Pharaohs had carried Egyptian blood in their veins. In the Second Intermediate Period Near-Eastern invaders had taken control of the Delta, and ruled as the Hyksos whom we have seen condemned by Hatshepsut. In the shadowy years following the collapse of the New Kingdom political unity was lost, and military officers of Libyan origin were able to seize power in several cities, again principally in the northern half of the country. But these were people who ruled Egypt from within, and they took pains to be seen as more Egyptian than the Egyptians, writing in hieroglyphs, worshipping the traditional gods, and organising themselves into dynasties. The Persian domination was different. In text-book language, the rule of Cambyses, Darius and Xerxes over Egypt is Dynasty Twenty-seven, but in practice this term is rarely used. The kings of Persia were Pharaohs within the country, and they paid lip service to Egyptian religion, but they ruled from Susa and Persepolis in Iran, and Darius and Xerxes were Zoroastrians, not devotees of Horus and Thoth. Effective control of the country was in the hands of a satrap, based in the natural capital, Memphis, but this officer was not allowed financial autonomy.

Economic affairs were administered by a separate chancellor, whose job included keeping an eye on the satrap and reporting to the king. Satraps had a habit of being recalled to Persia, to give an account of how they were running such a wealthy province. Like most powers in the ancient world, the Persians were tolerant of cultural diversity, and saw no reason to suppress Egyptian customs even if they had been in a position to do so. Egypt was able to hold on to its culture and religion, but it had lost much of its political independence. For the first time, it was part of an international state.

The country which the Persians absorbed into their empire had fought its way back to prosperity during the rule of the Twenty-sixth Dynasty (664–525 BC). This dynasty, like most in Egypt's history, ruled from Memphis, but it originated in the city of Sais in the Delta, and the period is often termed Saite as a consequence. Culturally, the period is marked by a revival of artistic, and to a lesser extent literary, motifs and devices which had flourished in the Old and Middle Kingdoms. In traditional works on Egyptology, this tends to be represented as a lifeless rehashing of unoriginal ideas, but some of this response is the result of our own unfamiliarity with Egyptian traditions as they would have seemed to those who were part of them. The Italian Renaissance is admirable to us, and rightly so, but this is partly because we are the heirs to it and understand its values. An alien from another culture, who did not understand the Renaissance from within, might compare it with the products of Greece and Rome and conclude that there was little that was new about it. Saite art is slowly being recognised for the rebirth that it was, although the period which produced it is still underrated.

Politically, the Late Period differs from most of Egypt's earlier history, in that there was invariably a hostile power on the country's north-eastern border. In the seventh century BC this enemy is Assyria, then it is Babylonia, and by the second half of the sixth century it is Persia. The first two powers succeeded in invading Egypt on several occasions, but neither was in a position to keep a permanent grip on the country. But the threat was constant, and the Saites needed to import military technology in order to counter it. Much of the expertise and some of the manpower which was required for this was to be found in the Greek world, and the Saite Pharaohs soon found that they were obliged to keep a balance between two forces: the need to open up their military structures on the one hand, and the necessity of placating the traditional army aristocracy on the other. The last group was severely jealous of its traditions and status, and a revolt among this caste would be disastrous. In the long run this balancing act failed, in that the country eventually lost its independence, but the ability of the dynasty to survive in what had become a very different world from that of the New Kingdom is still impressive.

The political skill of the Saite Pharaohs is underestimated, but there is another feature of the Late Period which is emphasised too often. Saite Egypt acted as a magnet for immigrants, who were drawn to the country for commercial reasons, or for military ones, although here too the fact that Pharaoh was one of the richest employers in the world would have played its part. Egypt became the home to large communities of Greeks, Anatolians, Phoenicians and the Aramaic-speaking tradesmen of the Near East, Jews, Libyans, Nubians and other Africans from further south along the Nile. As long as they obeyed the criminal and financial laws of the country, they could expect protection from the authorities. There was little or no racial prejudice, but there was strong pressure for such communities to assimilate to Egyptian culture. To be an Egyptian was to live in Egypt, and to worship Egyptian gods; where the individual, or the family, had come from was of minor importance compared with this. However, most textbooks, while noting the polyglot side to Saite Egypt, assume that it is a peculiarity of the Late Period. As far as we can judge, a similar state of affairs characterises the New Kingdom, and it may apply to the Middle Kingdom, if only on a smaller scale. In reality, it may hold true for Egypt at most of the periods of its long history. Many ancient Egyptians, and for that matter medieval ones, would have had grandparents or other relatives who had been born outside the country, and this is an aspect of Egyptian culture which is often overlooked.

The Persians inherited this state of affairs. Most of it was left untouched, but the Achaemenid rulers introduced refinements in several areas of Egyptian life. Aramaic, the *lingua franca* of the Near East, was brought in as the language of government. Coinage was introduced to what had been an economy based on barter and redistribution. Cotton, if it was not a Persian innovation, became a substantial crop in Egypt for the first time. One of the principal acts of Darius the Great when he seized power in 522 BC was to codify the law of the country as it stood in the last year of its independence, and the same ruler was responsible for digging the Suez canal. The idea of linking the Mediterranean with the Red Sea existed well before the nineteenth century AD, and may have existed in the nineteenth century BC; certainly there was a canal of sorts through the isthmus of Suez in the reign of Seti I, the grandfather of Prince Khaemwise. However, the Achaemenid version was designed on the scale appropriate to a world empire. One estimate of the volume of earth which was excavated for this project is 12 million cubic metres, and this does not include the freshwater wells which were also constructed. The canal was broad enough for two triremes to pass each other, and the southern section, between the Gulf of Suez and the Bitter Lakes, was lined with stelae inscribed in Iranian cuneiform and Egyptian hieroglyphs, each one listing the satrapies of the empire. Darius himself visited Egypt in 497/6 BC, during which time the waterway was formally opened. A flotilla of twenty-four ships was sent along the canal from Egypt, bound for Persia, and the Great King informs us as follows:

I ordered this canal to be excavated from the stream of the Nile, which flows through Egypt, to the sea which comes from Persia ... and ships sailed from Egypt through this canal to Persia, as was my wish.

This can be taken as the high noon of Achaemenid control over Egypt, and the blessings seem clear. Here is prosperity, and here is an international market, working for the well-being of all its citizens. This is the way that official sources would like us to picture the country, and they may not have been entirely wrong, at any rate as far as the governing classes and those who depended upon them were concerned.

The official picture may not be false, but it is not true either. There is always going to be a discrepancy between the rosy picture painted by government sources and the day-to-day functioning of the rest of a society; however, the state of affairs in the text known to Egyptologists by the pedestrian title of Papyrus Rylands IX introduces us to what appears to be another country all together. Yet this papyrus dates to the reign of the same Darius the Great who sailed his flotilla along the Red Sea. In this text there are no state openings, no international lawyers, and no superstate Pharaohs. As rambling accounts go of mismanagement, bankruptcy, petty corruption and family feuding in a small town in Middle Egypt in the sixth century BC, this document is in a class of its own. More than this, Rylands IX, or the Petition of Petiese as it is also called, is the single most informative secular text to come down from ancient Egypt. If it were not written in demotic, it would feature large in most of the textbooks, but, since it is, it is scarcely known outside the small group of scholars who enjoy working on this unprepossessing script. In the Saite period, there had originally been two administrative systems in use. Demotic was employed in the north of the country, where it originated, while a different script, known as abnormal hieratic, was in use in the south. Before the coming of the Persians, demotic had become the sole medium for

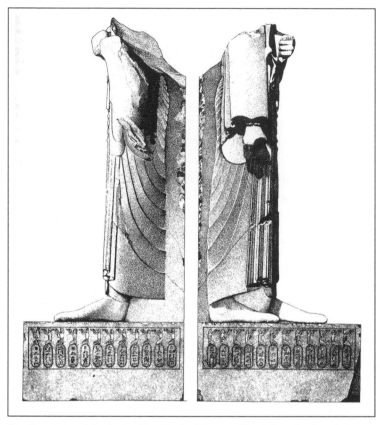

Headless statue of the Persian king Darius I (522–486 BC), found at Susa in Iran. On the base are the provinces of the Persian empire in Egyptian hieroglyphs. The statue was probably made in Egypt and shipped to Persia.

commercial and everyday communication in the Egyptian language. Early demotic is the most difficult stage even of this phase of the script, and the decipherment of the Petition of Petiese was the work of the scholar Francis Llewellyn Griffith. In 1909 Griffith published his three-volume catalogue of the demotic papyri in the John Rylands Library in Manchester. This catalogue is one of the masterpieces of Egyptology, and it is scarcely possible to improve on it almost a century later.

The Petition of Petiese begins in the month of July, 513 BC, when, almost in the style of a Western film, a stranger hits town. The town in question is called Teudjoy, and it was situated on the east bank of the Nile in Middle Egypt. The modern name for the site is El-Hibeh, but no tourists go there. The place had been of strategic importance in the Third Intermediate Period, when it functioned as a frontier post between rival territories, but by the time of Petiese it had become little more than a two-donkey town. The god of Teudjoy was the god Amun, who was once the patron of a great empire, and the name of the stranger is Ahmose, a priest of the temple of Teudjoy. Ahmose is an absentee priest, but he held the right to a stipend from the temple by virtue of his office. Priestly stipends could be sold from person to person in ancient Egypt, since they were a kind of share bearing a yearly dividend. Ahmose's dividend has not been paid for quite some time, and he wants to know why. The president of the temple explains to him that they are bankrupt, and the only solution will be to raise a loan. Ahmose inquires how this has come about, and is told that there is no one who can explain the state of affairs except the temple scribe, Petiese, son of Essemteu, who can give the history behind it all. The Petiese in question is the narrator of our document. By the time Ahmose came to town Petiese ('The gift of Isis') will have been about seventy. His sense of family history is strong, as is his sense of grievance. His memory for historical details is sometimes shaky, partly because of age, partly because much of his narrative is pieced together from family records. He will have had no access to an absolute chronology, and perhaps no king-list either. It is also fair to say that his sense of organisation is often absent, and he rambles across generations, returning to the same points repeatedly. But the story can be reconstructed, with some effort, and what he has to say is important.

Ahmose arrests Petiese and puts him on his ship, meaning to take him to the Persian chancellor in Memphis, adding, with the false bonhomie of the bully, 'I have refrained from beating you only because you are an old man and would have died.' When they reach the provincial capital, Petiese is made to stand in the sun until he comes out with an explanation of Teudjoy's financial ruin. Finally, exhausted by the sun, the old man calls for a roll of papyrus and writes down his statement. This has the effect of convincing Ahmose of Petiese's innocence, and he is released back to his own town. There the priests of Amun arrest Petiese over again, and he and most of his family are imprisoned. The temple president is sacked, and similarly imprisoned. There follows a touch which seems typical of such a backwater:

> On the 13 Mekhir [10 June 512], the festival of Shu, every one who was in Teudjoy was drinking beer, and the warders who were guarding us drank beer and fell asleep. Then Djebastefankh [the disgraced temple president] absconded. The warders awoke, but could not find him, and the warders who were guarding us also absconded.

One suspects that the warders too were not being paid, and absconding was a feature of peasant life in Egypt at most periods. The temple authorities then take the law into their own hands, beat Petiese and his family, and lock them up in a ruined tower near the temple gate, meaning to come back and demolish it on top of them. At the last moment it is realised that this will only bring down the wrath of the Persian authorities, and Petiese is sent back to his home, where he spends three months in the hands of the physicians.

What has wrecked this small town? The answer is much the same as we have seen in the chapter on the farmer Heqanakhte, although in his case the trouble is only beginning. At Teudjoy a feud, stretching back over generations, has poisoned the conduct of affairs in the temple, and the temple is the centre of the local economy. The origins of this feud can be reconstructed from the family archives which Petiese incorporates into his long petition. The point at issue is the known grey area between payments which are made to a person by virtue of his holding a particular office, and payments which are made to an individual *per se*. Both sides in this long-running dispute, the family of Petiese and the priesthood of the local god Amun, took advantage of the blurred edges which could result from such a system. The family of Petiese regarded payments made to their members from the temple of their small town as payments given to individuals, whereas the priests took the line that the money came by virtue of the offices held, and the holders of these offices were appointed by them. The priests were technically in the right, but they allowed their animosity to extend to benefits which really did belong to Petiese's family, and anyway the matter soon went beyond legal niceties. Petiese himself gives the impression of knowing that the truth was complicated, since his initial response to any query about the matter is extremely guarded. Over a lifetime he had learnt to be economical in his answers to officialdom.

The history begins in the early part of the reign of Psammetichus I, the founder of the Twenty-sixth Dynasty in particular and the Late Period in general. In the fourth year of this king (660 BC) the outgoing master of shipping, an important man in the resurgent administration, proposed to retire, and he named as his successor another Petiese, the son of Iturou, and the great-great-grandfather of the present narrator. This Petiese was a prodigy, who had managed to increase the wealth of Upper Egypt by half as much again. Pharaoh agrees to this appointment, and Petiese I, as we can call him, turns his attention to the affairs of Teudjoy, with which he had some ancestral connection. This temple, which had been wealthy when the place was a strategic one, had fallen on bad times.

(A recurrent pattern is visible here. Places like Teudjoy were not under royal patronage, nor were they economically self-sustaining. As a result, they were vulnerable to changing fortune.) Petiese I performs yet another economic miracle for Amun of Teudjoy, and in return is rewarded with a share of the priestly revenues, a contract which is witnessed by the local school scribe. According to the narrator, this priestly revenue was hereditary, and it passed in due course to Petiese I's son and grandson. There follows a romantic interlude, in which Petiese I's daughter becomes engaged to a young man named Haruodj, and the couple are rewarded by their patron, the retired master of shipping, with 'a wonder of a house, a house for a priest; there are no other classes of men within it, only priests and those who enter the temple'. Episodes of marginal relevance like this are characteristic of Petiese's style. They add to the colour of the document, but they can complicate things alarmingly. The old man likes to paint a broad canvas.

Things go reasonably well at Teudjoy until year 31 of the reign of the same Psammetichus (633 BC). The priests of Teudjoy take advantage of Petiese I's absence in Thebes to divert some of his stipend. 'As the sun god lives,' they say, 'Shall he continue to draw one fifth of the divine endowment? This outcast of a southerner is in our power.' The reference to people from the south is ironic, a comment on Petiese's absence in Luxor, but the notion that the south of the country is a joke persists in modern Egypt. Interestingly, when the priests of Teudjoy are themselves brought to the chancellor's court in Memphis, they too are dismissed in this way. The south of Egypt began quite far north, if one lived in Memphis, and this petition is full of passing insights of this sort. However, the matter quickly moves beyond a joke, since the priests target the two young grandsons of Petiese I:

> They charged some youths, evil-minded creatures, saying, 'Come with your staves in the evening, lie down on this emmer-wheat, and

hide your staves in it till morning' ... The two boys came to the temple, asking for their fifth part to be measured, but they [the young men] drew out their staves from the corn and surrounded them and started to beat them. They [the boys] fled from them into the holy place, but they [the men] ran up after them, and caught them, of all things, at the entrance to the shrine of Amun. They beat them to death, and threw them into a storeroom in the interior of the stone podium.

The disagreement over a stipend is now a blood feud. Things simmer on until the reign of Psammetichus II, almost two generations later. In the fourth year of this ruler (592 BC), preparations were set in motion for a campaign, or more likely a flag-waving exercise, in Palestine or the Phoenician coast. Representatives were to be sent from all the temples of Egypt, to carry garlands in the state procession. Who could be better qualified for such an honour that Petiese II, the grandfather of our narrator? This is what the priests maintain, and while Petiese is abroad representing his god, his colleagues set about redistributing the temple income according to their own view of the matter. Upon his return, the aggrieved Petiese II goes to the royal palace at Memphis to seek justice, but he is greeted with the words, 'Disaster: Pharaoh is sick, Pharaoh cannot come out.' (The reign of this king had only a few years more to run.) Eventually Petiese loses his case in Memphis, and returns to Teudjoy. A settlement of sorts is reached between the parties, and further litigation is discouraged with the following revealing words:

'There is nothing to be gained in going to the house of judgement. Your opponent in the case is richer than you. If there were a hundred pieces of silver in your hand, he would still defeat you.' So they persuaded Petiese not to go to the house of judgement.

Justice is expensive, in many societies. Our narrator then embarks on a lengthy discursus about events which happened in one of the following reigns, that of Amasis (570–526 BC). Here it emerges that the priests themselves were defrauded of part of their entitlement, when a superintendent of farmland sequestered some of the endowment of the temple. This dispute dragged on too, but it had the effect of reactivating the old feud with the family of Petiese, since the priests were looking for a scapegoat for their loss of revenue. They pulled down the house of Essemteu, father of our narrator, and turned their attentions to the statues and memorial stelae which Petiese I, the original benefactor, had set up on the temple platform. The statues, one showing the great man with a figure of Amun on his lap, and one which stood before a chapel of Osiris, were thrown into the river. One of the stelae was easily defaced, but the other turned out to be of granite. When the stonemason saw this he came out with the timeless excuse:

> I can't deface this. It's a granite-worker you need to deface this. My tools won't grip.

They leave this monument alone, and Petiese III includes a transcript of it in his petition. He quotes other inscriptions from the temple, and a series of oracles and hymns put into the mouth of Amun of Teudjoy about the need for justice and the punishment which awaits the evildoer. The language of these inscriptions is much more formal than that of the petition itself, and it is quite possible that Petiese has transcribed them accurately, although it would seem that his usual weakness when it comes to numbers has made itself felt, since some of the dates he gives are difficult to reconcile with others derived from monuments which we do have. But the documents quoted by Petiese perished centuries ago, and they survive only in this remarkable papyrus.

It is time to return to the main narrative. Petiese III is left to

Some of the lines from the petition of the old man Petiese. The script is demotic, a form of shorthand used for business documents during the Persian domination of Egypt. The papyrus is now in the John Rylands Library, Manchester.

recover from his wounds, and when he is well again he books a cheap journey to Memphis on a vessel carrying wood. He spends seven months petitioning the chancellor, who sends for the miscreant priests five times. On the fifth summons they deign to appear, and are punished with fifty lashes apiece. In the meantime they have succeeded in bribing the advocate who is supposed to be pleading Petiese's case, and they are allowed to go home without any further inquiry being made. Petiese manages to buttonhole the chancellor again one evening as he leaves his office, and he launches into his family history. Since this account would have resembled an even less coherent version of the one we have in the papyrus, the chancellor's reaction is understandable:

> These happenings which you are telling me are many. Why not take yourself to a house, take pen and paper, and write down everything which happened to your forefathers from the moment this share came into their possession. Write down the way in which the share was taken from your father together with the rest, and describe the events which have happened to you from that moment until now.

These are good stalling tactics. Unfortunately Petiese has reckoned without his corrupt friend at court, who succeeds in getting the whole matter dismissed with some vague assurances about letters being sent to everybody involved. Petiese returns to Teudjoy, but as he does so, he is met by some fellow-townsmen going north, who tell him, 'Are you Petiese? Are you going to Teudjoy? Do not bother; your house has been set on fire.' Petiese has no alternative but to return to the chancellor, who sends an agent to investigate further and bring back the priests who have done this crime. Eventually the agent returns, with a single suspect, who immediately denies everything. The suspect is given fifty lashes – clearly the standard gesture at the Chancellor's court – but the matter is left there. However, this cannot be the end of the affair, since Petiese is moved to recount the entire history of the family feud and his own misfortunes at the hands of the priesthood. The result is Papyrus Rylands IX, which was intended as a final petition to the authorities, perhaps to the satrap himself. The document was found among the ruins at El-Hibeh, along with the others now in Manchester, and it clearly never left the site where it was written. Perhaps a copy was sent to Memphis, and justice was eventually done, or perhaps Petiese's years got the better of him, and he went to join his fathers. Either way, the outcome is unknown.

We have only Petiese's account of events, and the priests of Amun would have had their own equally long version, but it is clear that we are not dealing with a society which functioned smoothly or followed principles of open government. Those of us who admire ancient Egypt might find this text embarrassing, and it is tempting to put the blame on the Persian occupation. The Persians, after all, would have had little interest in the affairs of a tiny town in Middle Egypt and the meanderings of an elderly man with a chip on his shoulder. But this buck-passing will not work. Petiese's ancestors met the same obfuscation and double-dealing at the courts of Psammetichus and Amasis, when Egypt was run by its own Pharaohs. The administrative texts from earlier periods, though incomplete and always partisan, nevertheless add up to a similar picture. This is a society which functioned intermittently, sometimes lubricated by bribery, at other times producing complete stalemates which could only be solved by arbitrary exercises of power. Unless such Gordian knots were cut, matters could fester over generations, and this could sometimes be the result whatever was done by the authorities. What makes such a society bearable is a sense of shared humanity, and a resort to ideals of harmony, even if such ideals are known to be elusive. What goes a long way towards making it unbearable is the refusal to lose face, and to abandon one's interest-group even when that group is the instrument of injustice and escalating violence.

The world of Rylands IX is the dark side of the tranquil texts which appear on the walls of Egyptian tombs. There the tomb-owner tells everyone who passes by about the life he led, giving bread to the hungry, water to the thirsty, clothes to the naked, and ferrying to the other bank the beggar who had no ferryman. Such people assure us that they never judged between two brothers in such a way that a son was deprived of his inheritance. These ideals were not empty, and Herodotus, who visited Egypt half a century after Petiese wrote his petition, remarks on the high standards of courtesy which he saw in the country. This was an aspect of Ma'at, the goddess of justice and harmony who was loved by Horemheb, and she was the daughter of the creator god. But the petition of Petiese shows that Ma'at could also turn her back on a place.

It is tempting to imagine that Petiese got to Memphis and found justice, inasmuch as his cause can be said to be a just one. We can think that he did, and we can also hope that his judge remembered the words of the sage Ptahhotpe, who wrote many centuries earlier:

> If you are one to whom petitions are made, listen with pleasure to what the petitioner says. Do not rebuff him, until he has poured out his heart, until he has said the reason why he has come. A suppliant would rather that his utterances were nodded to, than that the matter on which he has come should be settled. He rejoices in this, more than any petitioner. But as for someone who turns a petitioner away, people will ask, 'What does he mean by doing this?'

Perhaps Petiese had the fortune to meet with an official who had taken this worldly advice to heart. It is equally possible that he did not.

CHAPTER SEVEN

The Magician Pharaoh

Nectanebo II, reigned 359/8–343/2 BC

The history of ancient Egypt was measured not by kings and centuries, but by dynasties. By the middle of the fourth century BC the country had seen thirty such 'houses', as the Egyptians called them, and, if the gods were so minded, there was no reason why there should not be thirty more. Kingship had descended from heaven at the beginning of mythical time, and it had made its home in the city of the sun god, Heliopolis. If the rituals were performed properly, and if the embodiments of kingship who succeeded each other on the throne continued to rule in accordance with Ma'at and the demands of common sense, there would be no end to the system, short of a cataclysm which would put a stop to time itself. In addition, there were more practical arguments which could be brought in to reassure the nervous. Egypt was surrounded by deserts and seas, and was easy to defend, apart from the weakness of its north-east frontier, which needed constant watching. The country was naturally prosperous, at least when governed sensibly, and it attracted almost without effort entrepreneurial skills from less fortunate countries in the Mediterranean and the Near East. Younger nations marvelled at its monuments and the length of its history, although they tended not to imitate its culture, which was felt to be *sui generis*. The gods would surely go on protecting the land they had created.

With the perfect vision which comes with hindsight we can see that the gods had issued a series of warnings throughout the Late Period. The first millennium BC had not been Pharaoh's, in the way that the second and the third had been. There were considerable achievements to show for it, but the country had increasingly known the need to dance to others' tunes. The prosperity of the Saite dynasty had been followed by the first outright conquest of the country, and Egypt remained a province of the Persian empire from 525 until 404 BC, when it succeeded in regaining a precarious independence. The impact of this conquest on a proud civilisation was a complex mixture of passive aggression, Stockholm syndrome, profiteering, refuge in the country's history and traditions, and denial that anything out of the ordinary was taking place. In this way, even Cambyses, the Persian conqueror, could be made out to be the descendant of one of the Saite Pharaohs, in which case the so-called conquest was merely a kind of homecoming. In an entirely different tradition, the same Cambyses could become the murderer of the Apis bull and the enemy of everything sacred. Neither tradition has much chance of being true, but that is not the point: we have both versions, because they are attempts to come to terms with what had happened.

With the exception of the Greek city-states, Egypt was the first country to shake off Achaemenid control. However, when independence finally came, it did so at a price. The country was incapable of reasserting itself without foreign, and particularly Greek, expertise. Foreign observers had long suspected this to be the case, and now the Egyptians knew it too. This was a humiliation for a culture which prided itself on its likeness to no other. As it happens, the Late Period shows a concentration on precisely those aspects of ancient Egypt which made it different: the worship of animals, the distinctive cult of the dead, and the seemingly endless spirals of its theology. Yet this is also one of the periods which see Egypt becoming the host to foreign immigrants on a considerable scale. These two tendencies seem incompatible at first sight, but there is reason to suspect that they are linked. One way of dealing with a melting-pot of foreign immigration is to emphasise culture, and use it to override competing loyalties. This way, balance could be maintained, and the tension between the conservatism of the native aristocracy and the need to employ skills from outside this aristocracy could be defused. The question being addressed is, 'What does it mean to be Egyptian in this changing world?' The answer given by the ruling elite is to emphasise the points which make Egyptians unique. This policy worked with some success, and the story of most of the immigrant communities in the land is one of assimilation and absorption. A fine example of this can be seen in the story of Joseph, which, in the form in which we have it, dates to the Late Period. According to this, Joseph is a penniless immigrant, but he rises to the heights of fame and power by becoming more Egyptian than the Egyptians themselves. The lesson of this would not have been lost on the audience, since in the first instance that audience comprised men and women of Jewish extraction who had chosen to settle by the Nile. Joseph, the son of Jacob and Rachel, became an ancient Egyptian.

The Achaemenids never gave up their claim to Egypt, and this lent its own character to the period after 404. Using a modern analogy, there was a post-colonial mentality to the place. It may have been Egypt without the Achaemenids, but it was an Egypt where the idea of the Achaemenids was always present. Power passed into the hands of rival families, especially in the Delta, and the most successful of these warlords are the ones who are known to us as Dynasty XXIX. They may have been freedom fighters, but such people are not generally known for wanting to share their freedom once the struggle is won. Having a powerful enemy at the gates has kept many a historical regime in business. The new dynasty made the most of the constant threat from the former imperial power, by fostering the impression that they were the only people who could keep the Persians at bay. Conversely, the Persians encouraged the rivalry between the Delta factions throughout the rest of the fourth century. This in turn forced the princelings to develop links with powers outside the Persian empire, and in practice this meant the Greek world once again. Greek commanders and advisers became an essential part of the defence of the newly liberated province, but with a few exceptions these friends of Egypt did not come to the country in order to study its antiquities and admire the hieroglyphs. They wanted payment, preferably in hard currency. This meant that a country which was naturally short of metal needed to find the resources either to purchase coinage from abroad, or to manufacture its own. The resources for this could come only from the native Egyptians, and from the centres of wealth, chief among which were the temples.

After a quarter of a century of independence, power slipped from the immediate family of Dynasty XXIX to a distant relative, a military officer from Sebennytos in the central Delta who was named Nekhtenêbef. In traditional, Hellenised, terms this man is Nectanebo I, the first king of Dynasty XXX. If the previous dynasty can be characterised as a tissue of warlords, the following dynasty looks more like a military junta. This junta lost no time in appointing its own members to key positions. The message would be the same as before: the Persians are at the gate, and extraordinary times demand extraordinary measures. Trust the generals. An honest observer will admit that there was some substance to this, and the following generation saw defeats of the Persians whenever they tried to reinvade. No attempt was made by Nectanebo I to take the war into enemy territory, which would have exposed him both to military danger abroad and to political intrigue at home. The policy was to consolidate and to defend.

The wisdom of this approach was demonstrated beyond doubt in the following reign. In 362/1 BC Nectanebo I was succeeded by his son Djeho, known in Greek as Teos or Tachos. This prince lost no time in leading an amphibious operation against the Persian bases on the Phoenician coast, an area where the enemy was in enough difficulties with its own satraps to hold out a chance of success. The plan came unstuck, partly through its ambition, but partly through mutual suspicions within the army. We have the fragmentary autobiography of a priestly doctor named Onnofri son of Painmou, who accompanied the expedition, only to be denounced by means of a forged letter to his superiors. The atmosphere of intrigue and paranoia suggested by this inscription may well reflect the reality of the campaign. Another complicating factor was the rivalry which broke out between the young king and his principal military adviser, the king of Sparta turned soldier of fortune, Agesilaos. One expedition, however large, was not big enough for both these personalities.

Teos had undermined himself, at home as much as abroad. Acting on the advice of his financial pundits, who were all Greek, the king brought in new forms of taxation to finance his knockout blow against the Persians. One was a poll-tax, which proved as popular as poll-tax always does, and the other was an *ad hoc* levy on temple holdings. Pharaoh was the tax-raising authority in Egypt, and in theory he had the right to divert temple income to his own purposes, but in practice the policy was risky in the extreme, since it involved making an enemy of the scribal intelligentsia. To attack temples could be interpreted as a sleight on the gods, and therefore as hostility to everything which made Egypt what it was. Seen in this light, Teos was un-Egyptian. Some of the wealth raised by this stringent levy went into the minting of a series of gold coins, Greek in style but with Egyptian designs, which were intended to pay mercenaries. They are now collector's items, but it would have been better for Teos if they had never been coined. Most of the army in Phoenicia deserted to his nephew, a young man named Nekhtharnehbo. To us he is known, inaccurately but more pronounceably, as Nectanebo II, and he is the last Egyptian Pharaoh of Egypt. Plutarch, in his Life of Agesilaos, paints an unforgettable picture of the eighty-year-old king of Sparta addressing the new Pharaoh, who was sixty years his junior, as ô *neania* ('young man'), handing out unsolicited advice, and departing for Greece with a golden handshake of 220 talents. Pharaoh, even in his fourth-century condition, was still an employer to work for. But Pharaoh would not be going to Phoenicia again for quite some time, and the memory of Teos was quickly execrated by the priestly classes. He had fled to the old enemy, and sat there dreaming of revenge.

The hostility of Persia was understandable, but the affair of Teos will have reminded the more thoughtful among the Egyptians that they had as much to fear from Agesilaos and his fellow-countrymen, who were posing as their friends. Nevertheless, the ageing Spartan was able to do one last favour to the regime, by helping to put down a *coup d'état* in the Delta. Nectanebo was now the undisputed ruler, but the fate of his uncle Teos had taught him how precarious such a thing could be. Teos had not only taken on the gods, but he had run contrary to the spirit of the age. He had been impetuous, and to be impetuous was incompatible with being pious. Rashness and envy were the hallmarks of the god Seth, and this god was the everlasting enemy of Horus, the rightful heir to the throne of his father Osiris. Nectanebo sensed that, in order to survive, he must embody the spirit of the times, and become the self-image of Egypt, the country created by the gods to serve them and to enshrine their holiness. This may sound too rarefied to be convincing, but the Egyptians could envisage their country literally as the body of Osiris, divided into its parts by the power of his jealous rival, but still bringing forth life in spite of everything. What Nectanebo did was to make a virtue out of what had become a necessity, and this is as good a way as any of summarising his reign. We do not know whether he acted out of personal inclination or because of the needs of the moment; perhaps these two impulses coincided in his case. What is certain is that he was part of the military junta which had seized control of the country, but he adopted an image which to the modern mind seems completely at variance with such an origin. He becomes the dreamer of the Nile, the king who devoted himself to the traditions of a timeless Egypt, and the magician Pharaoh. The tired phrase 'a legend in his own lifetime' might have been freshly coined for Nectanebo, since this is precisely what he set out to achieve.

What the gods demanded from the king was piety, and one of the most effective signs of this mentality was the building of temples. All pharaohs were expected to add to the stock of religious plant, though some did more than others, either because of the resources available to them, or the length of their reigns, or as a consequence of personal religion, since particular monarchs could be drawn to particular combinations of gods, as we have seen in the case of Horemheb. Nevertheless, every Pharaoh would contribute something to the estate of the gods, even if it was only the rebuilding of a collapsed chapel or the adding of a few cartouches on a wall left empty by a predecessor. This was normal, but with Nectanebo II temple-building turns into an obsession. There are few sites in Egypt which do not show some mark of his activity, whether it be repair work, extensions to temples which had long existed, gateways, avenues, shrines or even whole new sanctuaries. The temple of Isis at Behbeit, near the seat of the dynasty, Sebennytos, was built entirely from scratch by Nectanebo II, and this was done, not in easy materials such as sandstone, but in the hardest granite. This policy had been begun by Nectanebo I, and in the temple-building stakes for ancient Egypt this king comes second only to Ramesses II. The latter, as we have seen, had sixty-seven years in which to put up monuments, whereas Nectanebo I had only eighteen. His great-nephew, Nectanebo II, was granted sixteen years by the gods, but there is no doubt that the combined building work of the Thirtieth Dynasty is one of the most impressive in Egypt's long history. It may even be the greatest, although the statistics of survival lend it an advantage which earlier dynasties have lost.

What lies behind this addiction to architecture? Temple-building was germane to ancient Egypt at most periods, and the Thirtieth Dynasty laid greater emphasis on piety than many. This provides something of an explanation, but there are deeper forces at work. One factor must have been the unsettling history that the country had been through in the previous century and a half. However it was interpreted, the trauma of conquest had left a mark on the Egyptians. One response was to take refuge in the country's long history, if need be by making it even longer. Herodotus (II 142), who had visited the land in the middle of the fifth century BC, calculated from the information given him by Egyptian priests that 11,340 years had elapsed from the time of the first recorded king until his own day. In the light of figures like these, what was a fleeting Persian conquest, and who, for that matter, did upstart Greeks like Herodotus think they were? The gods of the Greeks had their own names, to be sure, but anyone who looked upon the immense antiquity of Egypt would know that the true divinities were the Egyptian ones, from which it follows that the gods of the Greeks are merely the immemorial Pharaonic deities with newfangled names. Before the time of the first king, these gods had ruled over Egypt. Would protectors like these turn their backs on the land that they favoured above all others? At the same time, since the gods were wise and merciful, it follows that they must have tolerated the Persian conquest in order to inculcate a moral lesson. This lesson must be to do with piety; therefore it is time to turn back to the gods and redouble all efforts to placate them. This is what was expected of a Pharaoh, and Nectanebo was not the man to disappoint this expectation. It is no accident that the reign of this ruler saw the composition of an enigmatic text known to historians as the Demotic Chronicle, which survives on a papyrus now in Paris. This text records a series of oracles, which are interpreted to refer to the kings who preceded Nectanebo. In this work there is a clear link between the length of reign which a particular king enjoyed, and the attitude of the gods towards him. A typical entry runs as follows, elaborating on an excerpt from one of the oracles:

> The fourth ruler who came after the Medes was Psammuthis. 'He did not exist' means [that he failed] because he did not walk in the way of the god.

The moral of the Demotic Chronicle can be summed up as 'Honour the gods, that your days may be long', and this is what Nectanebo had every intention of doing.

It is in a similar spirit that we should see another of the innovations brought in by this dynasty. There are references in several texts of the period to the cult of the royal statues. There was nothing new about images of the king, but these particular statues were intended to be placed in the temples themselves, and they were given their own priesthoods and endowments. In this scheme, the disgraced Teos was replaced by his brother Tamos, the father of Nectanebo II. This is piety rendered tangible, and it is typical of the regime's use of propaganda. The junta was now on first-name terms with the gods. A more explicit use of propaganda was the growing cult of 'Nectanebo the Falcon'. The king of Egypt had always been a manifestation of Horus, and the falcon was the emblem of this god, but it is typical of Nectanebo to make this point literal. Horus had driven out the wicked Seth, and sent him into eternal exile. This is what had been done to the Medes, and it

A statue showing the youthful Nectanebo sheltering beneath the protection of a divine falcon. The scimitar and the pavilion in the king's hands, together with the falcon, correspond to the hieroglyphs which make up this Pharaoh's name.

was also the fate of Teos. Nectanebo the Falcon was the living symbol of the protection which Egypt continued to need and to receive. Another elaboration can be seen in a statue now in the Metropolitan Museum of Art, New York. This shows the king, still portrayed as youthful, holding a scimitar in one hand, and the hieroglyphic sign for a pavilion in the other. The king stands beneath the bosom of a large falcon. The whole is a visual play on the king's name, which means 'Strong (the scimitar) is Horus (the falcon) of Behbeit (the pavilion)'. Nectanebo II was one of the most image-conscious rulers that even ancient Egypt had seen.

The piety of Nectanebo's Egypt is a somewhat introverted quality, but introversion was what the times required. The temples were not simply landowners and homes for gods, but were also the seat of much of the intellectual life of the country. Under

Persian domination the learned classes had been forced to discover the virtues of adaptability, which they did, among other things, by claiming that most of the palaces of imperial Persia were the work of Egyptian craftsmen, or insisting that the only good doctors in the place were from their own land. Whole sections of the biography of Darius the Great were adapted to form the legend of Sesostris, the Egyptian who conquers the world. After the Persians had left, it took the combination of a quick wit and a low profile to prosper, perhaps merely to survive, in the unstable world of the Delta warlords. Quiet conformity, both to men and gods, was the way to live. The wisdom literature of the Late Period makes much use of the figure of the 'silent man', the person who walks in the ways of the gods, and avoids confrontation, exaggeration and dangerous impulses. Teos had not been a silent man, and Nectanebo could not afford to repeat this mistake.

Egyptian temples were not merely places for pious thinking. At most periods of the country's history, the temples were essential to the economic well-being of the land. We have seen examples of this elsewhere in these chapters. During the reign of Nectanebo II, the temple of Horus at Edfu in Upper Egypt owned the equivalent of thirty-seven square kilometres of land in its own province alone, and it could boast estates in other parts of the country as well. The temple of Edfu was far from being the wealthiest in the land. Some of these estates would have been owned outright, but others were usufruct from the Crown, which in theory owned all the land in the country and leased it out. (This can be taken as the hallmark of a primitive economy, though it is worth adding that the same is true of modern England.) Temples paid tax on leased land, and they also paid duty on manufactures such as textiles, papyrus, pharmacopoeia and metal-working. To invest in temple endowment was to build up the tax base of the Crown, and it was the Crown which had to pay for the defence of

Detail of the Metternich Stela, a magical text designed to secure dominion over the powers of anarchy and evil. The monument, which is a masterpiece of Late-Period sculpture, dates to the reign of Nectanebo II, and is now in the Metropolitan Museum of Art, New York.

the country. Older treatments of the reign of Nectanebo tend to see him as a Pharaonic version of Henry VI, squandering resources on unproductive piety and neglecting the politics of the day. In reality, religiosity and the economy went hand in hand, for the Thirtieth Dynasty as well as for its predecessors. It is notable that Cleopatra, whom nobody accuses of being ineffectual, did precisely the same thing, favouring the native temples and encouraging their economic expansion as a means of paying for the defence of the country and restoring its former glory. Handing out gold coinage to Greek mercenaries was not a popular move, but it was necessary. Piety was popular, and it was piety which minted the gold.

Nectanebo had another source of popularity, and he milked it for all it was worth. Magic was a component of Egyptian religion at all periods, since it was held to be one of the ways that gods communicated with men, and with each other. However, the fourth century BC was a good time to be a magician, since magic could be taken as an antidote to the vicissitudes of an unstable age. This is the heyday of the so-called healing statues, effigies of priests or other saintly figures which were decorated with hieroglyphic spells designed to heal physical illnesses, even moral deficiencies. The statues were kept in temple precincts, and most of them came complete with a basin which could be filled with holy water. This would be drunk by the pilgrim or suppliant, and the power of the inscriptions would then pass into his or her body. Statues of this type proliferate during the period, as do the stelae which are known as 'cippi of Horus'. These objects resemble boundary markers, and are sometimes made of green or grey schist, a stone which had numinous properties for the Egyptians. The inscriptions covering these stelae describe the victory of the god over serpents, scorpions and all the demons of this world and the next. (One of the finest examples is the Metternich Stela, which is also in the Metropolitan Museum of Art.) In these texts Horus – and for this deity it is not difficult to substitute Nectanebo the Falcon – is the master of all the terrors of the unknown. Since he can do this, he can easily handle the terrors of the known world, Persians included. Nectanebo was the high priest of Horus, as he was of all the gods, and he was therefore the embodiment of magic on earth. The story of the sorcerer's apprentice originated in ancient Egypt, and would have been current at this period. Would an apprentice want to be disloyal to such a quaint but faithful sorcerer as Nectanebo?

Egypt kept the Persian threat at bay until the summer of 343 BC. In 351 the enemy had mounted an attempt at invasion, but this failed, partly through a system of command and control which bordered on the farcical. The Persians were obliged to turn their attention to Phoenicia, which broke out in revolt following the débâcle.

Nectanebo's magic was clearly working as it should. Eventually, however, even this abundant resource let him down. The expedition of 343 was personally led by Artaxerxes, the Persian king, and it had learnt from the mistakes of the previous attempt. The Egyptians were outnumbered three to one. Pelusium, on the north-east frontier, was taken, and the ways to Memphis lay open. Treachery by some elements in what was still a divided army completed the story. The period of Persian rule was to prove short-lived, since it came to an end only twelve years later, when Alexander entered Egypt and was proclaimed Pharaoh. Hostile traditions paint a lurid picture of Persian atrocities within Egypt, which are certainly exaggerated, but the desire for revenge must have been present on the Persian side. Nectanebo fled the country, according to one source in the direction of Ethiopia. The temple of Edfu, which he had so richly endowed, continued to date events to his reign for a further two years, but in practice his rule over Egypt was at an end. A statue survives of the king's son and heir, but his name is lost, and there is no record that he was recognised as ruler; he may have been exiled or put to death by the conquerors. Nectanebo, as befits a good Pharaoh, had a magnificent sarcophagus prepared for himself, probably at Sebennytos or Behbeit. He was never to rest in it, and it was taken to Alexandria, where it was found by the Napoleonic expedition in use as a lustral basin in one of the city's mosques. It is now in the British Museum. After Nectanebo, no native Egyptian was to rule over the country until General Neguib, in the aftermath of the Officers' Revolution of 1952.

The gods of Egypt were unusual in that they promised immortality to their faithful worshippers, and Nectanebo too received his afterlife. The role of Nectanebo in tradition may not be as knockabout as Khaemwise's, but it is in some ways more evocative, since it derives from the medium of magic which he had done so much to make his own. It also became international. In Leiden there is a papyrus written in Greek by the hand of a teenager named Apollonios, in around 160 BC. The Greek settlers who flocked to Egypt after the arrival of Alexander sometimes took an interest in the literature of the native population, and translations of Egyptian writings were kept in the Library at Alexandria. The text copied out by the young Apollonios is called The Dream of Nectanebo, and the phraseology shows that it was originally composed in Egyptian. The story begins on the night of 5/6 July 343 BC, when Nectanebo, true to his reputation, has a dream. He sees the goddess Isis, the lady of the temple of Behbeit, accompanied by the enormous figure of the god Onuris, who was the lord of the city of Sebennytos, the dynastic home. The temple of Sebennytos has been neglected, and in particular none of the hieroglyphs has been inscribed. The god tactfully makes clear that this is not the king's fault, and the blame is laid at the door of a person named Samaus, presumably the temple administrator. Nevertheless, it is the Pharaoh's job to make things good. On waking, the king initiates a search for the fastest hieroglyph carver in the country, and this search throws up the name of a sculptor, Petesis. However, Petesis, like more than a few creative persons, turns out to be a heavy drinker. He manages to find his way to Sebennytos, somewhat the worse for wear, but there he sets eyes on the daughter of a street-vendor, who is the most beautiful girl he has ever seen. Unfortunately, here Apollonios the schoolboy scribe broke off, and took to doodling a picture of a man with a face which would still look like a face when turned upside down. We must guess the rest of the story. It may be that the hieroglyphs got to be duly inscribed, and Nectanebo's temple programme gloriously completed. Alternatively, the failure to meet the target may have been punished by the Persian conquest, since the date given at the beginning of the tale must be very close to the final invasion. Either way, it is likely that Nectanebo himself was exonerated; he had become too romantic, and too important a figure in Ptolemaic Egypt, to be permanently associated with failure in this way.

Exactly how important the last ruler of independent Egypt became in later legend is shown by an unlikely source, the Romance of Alexander. This Romance is a distillation of tales from a variety of sources which came together in Alexandria after the death of its founder in 323 BC. Many of its elements are Egyptian, as might be expected, and as a result we find that Nectanebo, the king who lost his kingdom, has succeeded in upstaging the legend of the greatest conqueror of all. This work was translated into many languages, and more people in the Middle Ages would have heard of Nectanebo, king of Egypt, than of Artaxerxes, the conqueror who replaced him. At the start of the Romance, Nectanebo is defending his homeland by means of a bowl of water and some model ships, which he animates and then sinks with his magic. For some reason this strategy turns out to be flawed, and the king disguises himself as an astrologer and settles in Macedonia. There he gains the friendship of Philip's queen, Olympias, who confides that her husband is anxious for a son. Olympias, both in the story and in reality, was well known as a bacchante, an initiate of Dionysos with an unhealthy obsession with snakes. Nectanebo promptly turns himself into a serpent, the age-old symbol of royalty among the Pharaohs, and in this capacity is invited into the queen's bed. The result is Alexander, who is passed off to Philip as the child of the god Amun, or Ammon. This neatly combines the historical link between Alexander and the oracle of Ammon at Siwa with the myth of the divine birth of the Pharaoh, which we have seen exploited by Hatshepsut. It also has the advantage of turning Alexander into an Egyptian, with the right to rule the country in his turn. Much the same had been done to Cambyses after 525: it was as if Egypt could only be conquered by one of its own sons.

The Egyptian king in the Romance is accompanied by a tame eagle which can send dreams, and this may well be an echo of the cult of Nectanebo the Falcon. He becomes the tutor to the young Alexander, assuming the role which in reality was played by

Aristotle. The would-be conqueror of the earth, however, begins to lose patience with his unworldly and mystical professor, and one day he throws him off a mountain into a pit. Here, Nectanebo has time to tell Alexander that he is his true father, whereupon, king or no king, he expires. The prince, overcome with remorse, buries the Pharaoh in the Macedonian capital. This may be a simple echo of the death of Philip, but the detail is a little strange. The text itself goes on to say this:

The end of the Greek text of the Dream of Nectanebo, written out on papyrus by the young Apollonios. The boy soon lost interest in the exercise, and took to doodling a childish figure with a face that can be viewed upside down as well as normally.

> It is a proof of divine providence that Nectanebo the Egyptian was laid to rest in Macedonia in a Greek tomb, while Alexander the Macedonian was to be laid to rest in an Egyptian one.

The facts about Alexander were known to everyone, but the information about Nectanebo seems gratuitous, since he could easily have conjured himself back to Egypt or anywhere else that tradition required. The story is fictional, but could this isolated fact be true? Philip was known to have ambitions on the Persian empire, and plans for an invasion of Asia were in place at the time of his death. A king of Egypt who wanted to have his world back could have done worse than to go to Philip's court, perhaps in the early 330s. Did Nectanebo remain there, and does he dream his dreams in the royal necropolis at Vergina, where Philip was laid to rest?

CHAPTER EIGHT

People of the Serapeum

Hor of Sebennytos and his companions, c. 200–150 BC

Few tourists who travel along the road from Cairo to the Step Pyramid at Saqqara pay attention to the desert *wadi* which runs west after the pyramids of Abusir, and fewer of those who visit the galleries of Khaemwise's Serapeum know that above their heads once lay a settlement, with its temples, shops, guest rooms for pilgrims and houses for many hundreds, now buried in the sand. This town grew up around the shrines of Graeco-Roman Memphis which were built on the escarpment overlooking the valley. Somewhere here lay the temple of Imhotep, who would answer to the name Asklepios, if people spoke to him in Greek. The whole settlement soon acquired the name of the Serapeum, and the characters who are the subject of this chapter lived in this area of the necropolis in the first half of the second century BC, five generations or so after the death of Alexander. Egypt was now ruled by Macedonian kings, and immigrants from most of the eastern Mediterranean flocked into the country, a story which was not exactly new. But the pull of Egyptian society, and particularly its religion, remained powerful, and many of these latest immigrants embraced the culture in which they found themselves, becoming Egyptian or semi-Egyptian in the process. The five subjects of this chapter may have been obscure, but their lives were affected by events which were momentous. The Ptolemaic kingdom in the second century BC went through an internal crisis, which saw the secession of Alexandria from the rest of Egypt and a shaky attempt to rule with two kings at once. This was accompanied by an external crisis, when the collapse of a bombastic crusade against the Seleucid empire in Syria led to defeat, invasion, and the humiliation of an appeal to Rome. Revolts sprang up in the south and in the Delta. At times the Ptolemaic state, whose wealth had seemed limitless, came close to bankruptcy. It is appropriate to such unsettled times that our characters seem to come out of darkness and to vanish into it. The papers of four of these people, which were unearthed somewhere at Saqqara in the early part of the nineteenth century, cover the years from 168 to 152 BC. A few are now in Cairo; the rest are scattered among the museums of Europe. The main source for these is the monumental first volume of Ulrich Wilcken's *Urkunden der Ptolemäerzeit* (always abbreviated UPZ), a work which has never been superseded.[2] The fifth is a discovery of the Egypt Exploration Society, who came to light in the 1960s and 1970s, a century and a half after his companions.

The first character is named Ptolemaios. We know something about his origins, but not as much as we would like. In a letter written in 159 BC he says that he has grey hairs, so he may have been born before 200. His birthplace was the village of Psichis in Middle Egypt, his father, Glaukias, a Macedonian soldier settled there as a veteran. Legally, Ptolemaios was a 'Macedonian by descent', or Egyptian-born Greek as native documents translate the term, and as such he describes himself when writing to the king. Somewhere around his thirtieth year he became a recluse, or *katochos*, in the Serapeum at Memphis. The nature of this strange title is uncertain. Some commentators argue that a man became a temple recluse for economic or social reasons, and it is possible that recluses were given licences to beg. Poverty may well have had something to do with the decision, but other writers, along with

Wilcken, prefer a mystical or spiritual interpretation. The two explanations may not be incompatible, but the point to emphasise is that a *katochos* was not allowed to leave the temple in which he was confined. As far as we know Ptolemaios lived the rest of his life in a cell – *pastophorion* – in the shrine of the Syrian goddess Astarte by the great Serapeum itself, and when his papers come to an end on 20 September 152 he is still 'held fast' by his god. Yet he always seems to have thought of Psichis as his home, as is shown by the text of a petition to the king which he wrote in 161 or 160 on the subject of his family:³

> To King Ptolemy and Queen Cleopatra from Ptolemaios, a recluse in the great Serapeum of Memphis for the past twelve years. In the month of Thoth in year 18 [October 164] my father, a native of Psichis in the nome of Heracleopolis, died, leaving myself, in the aforesaid temple, and three brothers, Hippalos, Sarapion and Apollonios, in the said village. Now news has reached me that they are being maltreated by the authorities in the village. I beseech you, Saviour and Benefactor gods, to look upon me, for I may not leave the temple to help them, and upon them, for they are orphans. Write to Cydias the provincial governor to ensure that no one in future maltreats or abuses them, for they provide the bread for my maintenance. And may it befall you to rule over every land that you desire, and to grow old with your children, and may your country flourish as you wish. Farewell.

Such protectiveness is a strong trait in Ptolemaios' character. His motives are not entirely altruistic, but that does not mean that he was not sincere. The habit of writing to the king went a long way back in Egypt, and Ptolemaios took to it assiduously. Ptolemaios kept the preliminary drafts of his letters, which are full of misspellings and alterations, while the final copies were sent to the recipients and are lost. In another letter, written in October

164, he shows his concern for a girl who had come into his life in some way:[4]

> To the kings: Ptolemaios son of Glaukias, who for the past nine years has belonged to those who are in confinement in the great Serapeum of Memphis. In year 7, month of Thoth, a certain person named Heracleia took refuge in the aforesaid sanctuary and became my servant. Because I have no children I adopted [?] her. But Zoilos, a mace-bearer from the temple staff, obtained the wherewithal from certain persons and seized the girl, and because I was unable to leave the temple he handed her over to one of the soldiers from Memphis. Therefore I beg you, O greatest gods, Saviours and Benefactors, not to overlook his attempt to enslave this Heracleia, not to mention his abduction of her contrary to all that is right.

The result of this petition is not certain, nor are we quite sure what is going on. The word 'adopted', which was suggested by the gentlemanly Wilcken, may be a wrong translation, and Ptolemaios might have been intending Heracleia to become the mother of children of his own. However, we hear nothing about any such children, and there were to be no more Heracleias in Ptolemaios' life. A point which soon becomes clear is the contrast between the confinement of this man, which he is always stressing, and the way in which his mind voyages beyond his walls, seeking to protect outsiders, on occasions almost to control them. This is a conflict to which we will return. Whatever the truth, one might imagine that the life of a temple recluse was monotonous and free from incident. It was not, as another petition shows:[5]

> On the 16th of Thoth [18 October 163] Ptolemaios, the agent of the chief of police in the Anubicion, and Amosis, the deputy of the high priest, entered the shrine of Astarte where I have been

confined until the present, accompanied by policemen. They claimed that there were arms hidden in the place, and instituted a search of the entire building, but found nothing. The policemen kept up a commotion by the exit, but nothing untoward occurred. Eventually, at a late hour, Amosis returned with Imouthes, the agent of the overseer of subsidiary priests, and Harendotes and others, carrying a lamp. He laid violent hands on me and proceeded to plunder the shrine, carrying off all that was portable and putting a seal on the rest. On the 17th of the same month he returned early in the morning and carried off the remainder which was under seal, and even went so far as to plunder the savings of the other recluses. But one Harmais recognised his jar, in which money was kept, and seized hold of it. Amosis was not deterred at all, but put a seal on this too ... Why, he even entered the holy of holies of the goddess and ransacked that, practically demolishing it. Finally he returned again, this time with Harimouthes the agent of the temple inspector, and discovered a bronze vessel belonging to the goddess, which he removed. In addition to this, Pabelphis son of Peteharendotes and Nekhtenibis son of Imouthes without any propriety entered the shrine, searched it, failed to find anything pertinent, caught sight of a few lead cups, and decided not to leave these either. I asked them why they had come; they replied that they had been sent as bailiffs ... Therefore I beg you, O king, not to abandon me to the onslaughts of these accused, but, if it please you, to accept as my counsel Demetrios son of Sosos the Cretan, for I myself may not leave the shrine, and to set the accused before you, that they may make amends to me before your judgement-seat. If this happens I will have experienced your salvation. Farewell.

Ptolemaios had cause for worry. Many of his papers deal with economic matters: affairs of the house in Psichis, which seems to have been burdened with joint mortgages, and his own precarious finances. He received, at least in his last two years, an allowance of

100 drachmas a month from the temple authorities, but this clearly did not go far. He had sidelines, in particular dealing in pieces of linen and a distinctly strange trade in a sort of porridge, but these activities may have made him enemies in the necropolis. Like other recluses, he minded sums of money on behalf of others. Sometimes he sells off possessions – on one occasion even a cow – to make ends meet. Constantly petitioning the king would have had its hidden costs, in payments to petty officials. Much of his income seems to have been spent on his protégés, and on occasions he sinks into despair. In another text he cries, 'My spirit fails me because of my confinement and because of (his ward) Tawê. On what shall we live?'[6]

There are other sides to this kindly but troubled man. He was educated, and it may be that he identified being literate with being Greek. Somewhere he acquired a book on astronomy, attributed to Eudoxos of Knidos, and wrote his own notes in the margins of it. Two epigrams on the Pharos lighthouse and the temple of Arsinoe Zephyritis outside Alexandria would have been lost to us if it had not been for Ptolemaios' ungainly hand, and one day he caused to be written out several lines from Euripides' *Medea*, a strange product of this desert place. The lines are about the anguish of exile to a foreign land. When we last see Ptolemaios he is hoping as ever for his release, but this does not come.

The second character is more fiery. He is the youngest brother of Ptolemaios whom we have already met in the house at Psichis, and he is the adolescent who copied out the opening lines of the *Dream of Nectanebo*. The difference in the ages of the two brothers is so great – perhaps as much as thirty years – that Apollonios sometimes refers to Ptolemaios as his father, and at a deeper level this may have meant more than convention. Glaukias the soldier was dead, and Ptolemaios was now the head of the family. Before long, Apollonios is found acting as his brother's secretary, and his handwriting is certainly the better of the two, although his spelling shows that he spoke Greek with an Egyptian accent. He also knew how to write demotic, and his Egyptian spelling is so much better than his Greek that one wonders whether this was not his first language. This makes it likely that Apollonios' mother was Egyptian. Given the difference in ages, it may be that Apollonios is the child of a second wife, in which case he is strictly Ptolemaios' half-brother. But this is never said, and it is possible that both brothers had the same mother, which would mean that Ptolemaios too was partly Egyptian. This hybrid element in Apollonios' make-up goes some way to explaining his touchiness about his origins. He complains constantly about ill-treatment from the Egyptians who surround him, although the chances are that they were severely provoked. Nevertheless, the feeling is sometimes shared by Ptolemaios: 'People here abuse me,' the elder brother says, 'because I am a Greek.' In the cramped and overcrowded Serapeum, with the uncertainty of political events, quarrels must have been frequent. We shall return to Apollonios' racial feelings, but they are not the only complication in this volatile character. In particular, he shows an ambivalence towards the religious beliefs which preoccupy his elder brother, and he is sometimes near revolt. The tone of much of his writing is shown in the following account:[7]

> To Poseidonios the royal friend, herald and governor, from
> Apollonios son of Glaukias, a Macedonian. I happen to be in
> detention in the great Serapeum in Memphis. In year 23, 25 Paoni
> [23 July 158] I went to the bulrush-shop which is attached to the
> said shrine to buy some reeds [used for fuel]; but the seller refused
> to sell the ones he normally sells to all his customers, trying to
> force on me others of a substandard variety. I demanded to buy the
> decent ones, which he gave to me in a threatening manner; I took
> them and went back to my cell. Later, however, the shopkeeper's
> sons, Petaus and Teos, arrived carrying staves, and without any

decency charged into the cell where I live. They insulted me and thrashed me with their staves, since they are donkey-boys, extorting money in addition to what they had already obtained. Neither the [sanctity of the] temple nor the law deterred them. For these reasons I take refuge with you and urge, if it please you, to summon them so that I may obtain justice.

The quarrel between Apollonios and the sons of the shop-keeper was studied in the 1930s by an Egyptologist named Nathaniel Julius Reich, who had emigrated from Europe to the United States. This eccentric character stands in marked contrast to the magisterial Wilcken. Reich makes constant blunders in hesitating English, Wilcken's prose is tight with scholarship; yet it is Reich who is the better interpreter of Apollonios, for he understood this rootless adolescent in a way that was not available to Wilcken. He also showed that Apollonios must have been in the wrong in his quarrel with the shopkeeper, and that the boy's youth had got the better of his circumspection.

A strange turn of events appears in this letter, since Apollonios is now calling himself a *katochos* like his elder brother. This state of affairs lasted a mere eight months, from February to September 158, and it is typical of the younger man to leap in and out of an institution from which Ptolemaios can find no release. If economic circumstances forced this action, it is surprising that neither brother makes any mention of them, whereas if the *katochoi* were driven by an inner compulsion the matter becomes extremely difficult to chart. The psychological explanation may turn out to be the right one, but it raises questions which are at present insoluble.

Ptolemaios, it will occasion no surprise, is soon planning an entirely different future for his brother. A decision is made, Ptolemaios tells us by himself, to place Apollonios in the army, which had been the father's profession. A day by day account is contained in a long document, UPZ 14. The affair began simply on 3 October 158, when Ptolemaios, not for the first time, wrote to the king. The petition is thrown by Apollonios, who has regained his liberty, through the window of the nearby Anubieion, where the king was staying during a state visit. The king's immediate reaction is not recorded, but the petition is soon returned with a comment, either in the ruler's own hand or that of a scribe: 'Do it; but report back how much it will cost.' Apollonios then carries the document to Demetrios the quartermaster, who instructs a deputy to draw up the necessary information. There follows an excruciating list of reports to departments, sub-departments and secretaries, together with memoranda to each giving full details of the circumstances and copies in triplicate to be addressed to the army officials, the Memphite authorities and the pay corps. Eventually, in February 157, Apollonios receives his papers, which

> were delivered to be read to the chancellor, and I received back the decree from Ptolemaios the memorandum-drafter and the letter from Epimenides. And I conveyed them to Isidoros the *autoteles* and from him I carried them to Philoxenos and from him to Artemon and from him to Lykos, and he made a rough draft, and I brought that to Sarapion in the office of the secretary and from him to Eubios and from him to Dorion, and he made a rough draft, and then back again to Sarapion. And they were handed in to be read to the chancellor and I received them back from Epimenides and I carried them to Sarapion and he wrote to Nicanor; and Nicanor wrote two letters, one to Dorion the *epimeletes* and one to Poseidonios the governor of the Memphite nome.

We have met ancient bureaucracy elsewhere in these chapters, and it is gratifying to see that the Greeks were able to perfect it in this way. Anyone who wonders why the Hellenistic monarchies folded up at the arrival of the Romans may like to read UPZ 14.

After all this, Apollonios received a posting of sorts, but it appears to have been unpaid, and he turned to supplementing his income as a police informant, a job which literally gave him nightmares. This rather shady outcome may explain some of the hostility that both brothers attracted in the Serapeum. The relations of Ptolemaios and Apollonios with the authorities seem to have been close, and this could well have made them suspicious, especially to the Egyptians who surrounded them.

The next characters come together, which is appropriate, since they are twins. Taous and Tawê are the daughters of an Egyptian who had been a friend of Ptolemaios the Greek. An account of their early life is contained in UPZ 19. The woman named Nephoris is their mother:

To King Ptolemy and Queen Cleopatra, the gods Philometores, greetings. Taous and Tawê, the twins who serve in the Memphite Serapeum, pouring libations to Serapis for you and your children. We are grievously wronged by Nephoris and her son Pakhrates, and take refuge in you to find justice. The said Nephoris left our father and went to live with Philippos, a soldier from Memphis. Then she arranged for Philippos to make an attempt on his [our father's] life. He sat himself by the door of his house, which lies by the river near the Egyptian market, but as our father came out he realised what was happening and scrambled into the river. He managed to escape to an island, where he was rescued by a passing boat; but he could not bring himself to return to the bank, and went instead to the nome of Heracleopolis, where because we were no longer with him he died of grief. His brother sailed upstream and brought back his body to the Memphite necropolis, but to this day Nephoris has not troubled to bury him. His belongings, which had been deposited in the royal treasury, were appropriated by Nephoris, and she sold one half of the house – though it was ours as well as hers – for 7 talents of bronze. She acquired a property worth 60 talents and draws a monthly rent of 1,400 drachmas from this, but she gives us no share. Not content with this, she threw us out, and we faced starvation. But a certain Ptolemaios, one of the recluses in the Serapeum, who had been a friend of our father's, took us in. At that moment the mourning for the Apis was declared, and they hired us to make the lamentations for the god ...

Thus the chance death of an Apis bull on 6 April 164 BC meant a change of fortune for the twins. We are still in ancient Egypt, even if letters to the authorities are now in Greek. The twins had a job, impersonating the goddesses Isis and Nephthys, and their duties were presumably light, but this was not the end of their troubles, since Pakhrates, their half-brother, succeeded in embezzling their salary. Many of the papers of Ptolemaios are concerned with the financial affairs of these Egyptian girls, about whom he is constantly worrying.

It is rare to be able to enter the minds of any people, ancient or modern, but the characters of the Serapeum are exceptional, because all four of them have left us accounts of their dreams. Ptolemaios wrote his dreams down in Greek, while those of the twins are in demotic, as one would expect. Apollonios also shows a preference for the Egyptian language. Dream-texts are notoriously difficult to interpret, but it is impossible not to be drawn into this sort of thing when confronted with such confiding material. Here is a miscellany from the hand of Ptolemaios:[8]

The dream which Tawê the twin saw on 17 Pakhons [15 June 161]. She dreamt that she was walking along the street, and counted nine houses. I wanted to turn back, and said, 'These make nine at the most.' They said, 'Yes; you are free to go.' I replied, 'It is late for me.'

The dream which Ptolemaios saw on the festival of the moon on 25 Pakhons. I dreamt I saw Tawê speaking well, with a sweet voice

Stela of a dream interpreter, from the Serapeum at Saqqara. The Greek text runs, 'I judge dreams, having a commission from the god. Good fortune. A Cretan is the one who interprets these things.' The irony is that Cretans in the ancient world had a proverbial reputation for being liars.

and in a happy spirit, and I could see Taous laughing and her foot well and whole.

The 29th. Two men are working in the forecourt, and Taous sits on the stairs and jokes with them; then she hears the voice of Chentosneu and immediately turns dark. They said they would teach her [...].

The dream of Ptolemaios on 15 Pakhons [13 June 161]. Two men stood next to me, saying, 'Ptolemaios, take the money for the blood.' They counted out for me 100 drachmas, but for Tawê the twin bronze staters, a full bundle. They say to her, 'See the money for the blood.' I say to them, 'She has more money than me.'

Year 23, 4 Pakhons [2 June 158]. I dreamt that I called upon the great god Amun to come to me from the north with his two consorts, until finally he came. I dreamt that I saw a cow in that place in labour. Amun seizes the cow and flings it to the ground; he thrusts his hand into her body and brings forth a bull. What I saw in my dream, may it be well with me. 23 Pakhons, my birthday.

This is as labyrinthine as dreams can be, but certain themes are clear. Ptolemaios seems to interpret the birth of the bull in the final dream to mean that he will be released from his confinement, and the same longing may lie behind his words in the first dream. It is also striking to see the complexity of his feelings towards the twins, some aspects of which he would never have admitted consciously. The second dream shows his clear concern for their well-being, but the third dream reveals an irritation that the sister Taous is not under his control, an emotion which may have a sexual element to it. A certain jealousy directed against the other twin seems to lurk in the fourth dream, and an impatience, again with Tawê, blows through the opening scene. Such reactions need not be permanent: they may have been the results of trivial, passing, incidents, and one of the functions of these dreams would have been to release the tensions of an enclosed life.

There is none of this subtlety with Apollonios; he comes straight to the point, and in Egyptian:[9]

The first dream: I am walking along the avenue of Serapis with a woman called Tawê, who is a virgin. I talk to her saying, 'Tawê, is your heart troubled because I seduced you?' She replies, 'It happens that Thotortais [and] my sister are angry with me, saying that I have become a whore [?].'

The second: A singer sings, 'Apollonios speaks Greek, Petiharenpi speaks Egyptian; the one who knows is this priest.'

The third: I am in my house with my elder brother. He is weeping before me, saying, 'I have ceased my blessings, and my hand has passed them by.' I reply, 'Do not be afraid ...'

The fourth: I find a man who has come as a rebel to the place of asylum. What he said was, 'The goddess Sekhmet told me to touch the lamp in the Serapeum, and this made all my men delay.' I replied, 'They will not oppose you because of the lamp. They will be pleased with you at first, but you will suffer a setback when they start an investigation.'

Several aspects of Apollonios are revealed here. He appears as more helpful towards others than his public *persona* would suggest. He has some kind words for the rebel, and he tries to comfort his elder brother in his despondency, although this may be a reversal of the normal state of relations between the two. Ptolemaios can never have entered the house where Apollonios lived, so at least one aspect of this scene is fictional. The opening dream is the most vivid: the apparently gratuitous information that Tawê is a virgin is given to deny the force of the words which follow. Apollonios did not seduce Tawê, and virginity was a requirement for the ritual office that Taous and her sister occupied. The second dream, though short, is very revealing. It brings to the fore the preoccupation with trying to reconcile the two races which is one of the young man's greatest problems. Petiharenpi is the Egyptian equivalent, or translation, of Apollonios, and it is almost certainly the name he went under when speaking Egyptian. Perhaps it is close to being his real name. However, it is the final dream which tells us most. Here the young man meets a rebel who is delayed by a religious scruple, and this is as good a definition as one could wish of the character of Apollonios. In this dream, he comes near to analysing himself. The final speech is remarkable. The words could mean that the conflict which is at the base of his personality can be resolved temporarily, but in the long run, 'when they start an investigation', a crisis is inevitable. But this is difficult ground, and it is simpler to move on.

The dreams of the twins have a quieter tone. The following are written in demotic on a potsherd, and are now in St Petersburg. We do not know which sister is speaking:[10]

> The first dream: I saw myself in Memphis. I dreamt that the water had flooded up to the statue of Wahibre. My mother was standing on the bank. I cast off my clothes and threw them up into the sky. I swam towards her, to the eastern side. I took some more clothes from Taanupi the washerwoman, and spoke to her saying, 'This is the second time that I have crossed over to you. I ferried over to you before – see, there is the landing-stage. I did it and I lodged safely in your house.' She greeted me with the words, 'I have the receiving of you.'
>
> Another dream: I found myself in the house of Shepanupi. I dreamt that he had married the woman Tsenqaie. They spoke to him, saying that he loves her. But I replied myself, 'She loves her mother, while his heart loves the one whom he loves' ... Written in year 21, Mesore, day 6 [2 September 160].

The most obvious feature of these dreams is the preoccupation with the mother. In the first, it is not easy to decide whether the person being addressed is the mother or the washerwoman, but one can be forgiven for wondering whether it makes much difference. Particularly moving is the twin's reception into the house from which in reality she had been excluded. Wilcken, charitable as ever, concluded that this dream was history, and that there had been a reconciliation between the twins and their mother, but it is more likely that we are dealing with wish-fulfilment. The river bank appears in the dream, as it might, since this was the scene of the murder attempt on the twins' father. The next dream is also revealing: marriage was presumably a subject which occupied the minds of Taous and Tawê, and one wonders whether butting into conversations was also characteristic of them. Once again the mother intrudes into their thoughts.

The twins, however, are mostly seen through the eyes of others. The most vivid impression comes from a letter of Ptolemaios to his friend Damoxenos, which he dictated to his younger brother:[11]

Year 22, 12 Tybi, running into the 13th [night of 10/11 February 159]. I dreamt I was in Memphis walking from west to east, and stumbled over a pile of hay, and a man came towards me from the west and also stumbled over it. My eyes were as it were sealed; but suddenly I opened my eyes and saw the twins in the school of Tothes. They called out. I said, 'Take care not to be faint hearted. Tothes will find it difficult to track me down, for I have changed my bed.' I heard Tothes say, 'Get out of here immediately. What are you saying? I will bring the twins to meet you.' Then I tell you I saw him bring them. I walked in front of them, to seize them, and I stepped with them into the street. I told them, 'I have only a short time in the world, and soon everything I was [will be no more].' But immediately I saw one of them running off to a nearby house, where she squatted and urinated; and I saw that the other one had gone ... And I saw many other things, and once again I prayed to Serapis and Isis, saying, 'Come to me, lady of the gods, show grace and listen to me. Have mercy on the twins, for you instituted them as Twins [in the Apis rituals]. Release me; behold my grey hairs, for

I know that in a short time I shall be dead. But they are women, and if they are defiled, they will never be pure again.'

On the 14th I dreamt that I was in Alexandria, on top of a high tower. I had a beautiful face, and did not want to show my face to anyone, because it was beautiful. An old woman sat by me, and a crowd gathered from north and east. They cried out that a man had been burnt to ashes [...], but she said to me, 'Wait a little, and I will take you to the guardian-spirit Knephis, so that you may worship him.' And in my dream I said to one of the elders, 'Father, did you not see this vision which I saw?' I described it to him. He gave me two reeds. I looked up suddenly, and saw Knephis.

Be joyful, all who are with me; release is not far off. I have seen other things, even finer. You know that my aim is for the twins to find a safe harbour. I am not worried about anything else ... Send for the twins and tell them that I am coming out. Amosis has come to me, he has shown me the way, and has opened the doors of the shrine before me.

It is impossible not to be moved by the power of these words, but an outsider might also wonder whether Ptolemaios was sane. It is true that the religious system that he lived under is alien to a modern mind, but this in itself does not make a person insane. There are many things we do not know about Ptolemaios, but his behaviour is not wildly unpredictable. The large number of economic papers he has left show a mind in control of itself, if a little obsessed with detail, and in general it is unlikely that the *katochoi* were confined lunatics. It may even be that dreams of this sort were the things which kept him sane. It is more profitable to see how his character unfolds in this letter: his concern for the twins, combined with a fear of their independence, his pessimism, followed by fits of optimism which protest too much, and his self-effacing exhibitionism. 'I had a beautiful face, and did not want to show my face to anyone, because it was beautiful.' Beautiful faces could be a sign of divinity in the ancient world, but, lurking beneath this, is the paradox which makes Ptolemaios write letters to the king on behalf of a family from which he hides himself. Incidentally, most of his predictions were wrong: the god did not let him go, and in spite of his grey hairs he was still alive seven years later.

Apollonios must have found his brother complex, but the violence of his rejection, when it finally came, is unmistakable. The incident which prompted the following letter is obscure, but the real issue is clear. The date of UPZ 70 is around 156 BC:

Apollonios to Ptolemaios his father greetings. I swear by Serapis, if I had not a sense of shame, you would never see my face again. Because you lie in everything, and the gods who are with you lie also, and because you have thrown us into a great mire where we may die, and whenever you 'see' that we are on the point of being saved, it is then that we sink. Know that the fugitive will try to upset everything, for thanks to us he has been fined 15 talents. The governor is coming up to the Serapeum tomorrow, and will spend two days feasting in the Anubieion. But there is nowhere in Trikomia that I can hide my face for shame at the way we have sold ourselves and stagger along deceived by the gods and believing in dreams. Farewell.

In the left-hand margin of the note is scrawled the afterthought, 'Against all those who tell the "truth".' Trikomia is an uncertain place, but in this context it seems to be the equivalent of the world. Howard Carter, in his account of the opening of Tutankhamun's tomb, remarked on the bowl of mortar left by the door, the fingerprints on the wall, and the footprints of the mourners in the dust: things which annihilate time, and turn the observer into an intruder. This letter does the same, over twenty-two centuries.

Hor (or Horus), son of Harendotes, was a minor Egyptian priest. His writings, in this case on potsherds (ostraca) rather than papyrus, are similar to those of Ptolemaios, and contain much the same mixture of factual and spiritual, petitions and memoranda, accounts and dreams. They are all in demotic, apart from a small number in fumbling Greek. Although his documents were found at Saqqara, Hor originated in the Delta, in a town called Pi-Thoth in the province of Sebennytos, and he was trained as a priest of Isis in a nearby temple. He was probably born slightly before 200 BC, and is therefore a contemporary of Ptolemaios. Some time after 165 BC Hor received a divine instruction to settle in the ibis-shrine of the god Thoth near the Serapeum, and he became a neighbour of Ptolemaios and his wards. There is no proof that he knew them, apart from a small ostracon among his collection which mentions an anonymous pair of twins, but it is extremely likely, given the proximity of all five characters and the interests they shared. Hor of Sebennytos worked at the ibis-shrine as a secretary, and probably as an adviser on dreams and oracles, since he already had a reputation for such things before he settled at Saqqara. In his early life he became involved in national politics at a surprisingly high level, and here is his account of a dream which he experienced while he was attached to the Ptolemaic army during the invasion of Antiochos Epiphanes (Hor Text 1). This perilous event took place in 168 BC, and came to an end only after the Romans intervened.

> In year 23, Hathor [December 159] I reported to Soterion, the
> scribe of Pharaoh at Memphis, the matter which had come true
> when Antiochos was to the north of Pi-Eulaios and Egypt was torn
> apart. I spoke with Eirenaios, who was commander of the army and
> acted as representative for Pharaoh Ptolemy our lord. I caused him
> to realise the truth of the matters which I had discovered, the
> fortune of Pharaoh. The lady of the Two Lands, Isis, was the one

who ordained them, and the great god Thoth was the one who recorded them. I dreamt as follows: Isis, the great goddess of Egypt and the land of Syria, is walking on the face of the water of the Syrian sea. Thoth stands before her and takes her hand, and she reached the harbour at Alexandria. She said, 'Alexandria is secure against the enemy; Pharaoh is recorded within it, together with his brother. The eldest son of Pharaoh wears the diadem; his son wears the diadem after him; the son of this son wears the diadem after him; the son of the son of the son of this son wears the diadem after him, for very many lengthy days. The confirmation of this: the Queen bears a male child.'

This dream threw Hor into the midst of political events. His commander, Eirenaios, at first refused to believe all this Egyptiana, but when Antiochos was forced to retreat, he began to take his prophet more seriously, even arranging an interview for him with the two Ptolemies and the Queen. This took place in the Serapeum in Alexandria on 29 August 168, and it is an unusual testimony to how mobile Egyptian society could be at this period. Finally, Eirenaios began to write for his Egyptian friend letters of credential. This conversion of Eirenaios is an individual example of an important movement in the history of thought: the orientalising of the Greeks. To earlier classicists such as Gilbert Murray or E. R. Dodds this reversion appeared as a failure of nerve, but to an Egyptologist it looks more like a homecoming. The fusion of Egyptian religion with Greek philosophy began at places like Saqqara, and the god of Hor, Thoth the three-times great, became Hermes Trismegistos, celebrated as the font of pagan learning even down to the Renaissance.

Hor's gods did not desert him, but began to drive him south, to Memphis. The following text is in some ways the common denominator of this final chapter:[12]

Painted shroud from Memphis, dating to the late second century AD. This shows the deceased as a young man wearing a tunic and mantle, flanked by the jackal-headed Anubis, guide to the next world, and the full-face figure of Osiris, ruler of the Afterlife.

Day 12, festival of Thoth. The first dream: I dreamt that a young
master [overseer] was with me on a labour-gang, and had paid my
exemption money. I dreamt that I absented myself, but they came
after me and brought me to a halt in Sebennytos. They brought me
to the place where my master was. I was very afraid. My master took
me to the temple, and said to me, 'Hor, you are on trial; I shall keep
silence, and you will find that this is a serious charge. You must go;
you may not stand before me. I am your master: Thoth. I told you
before, "Do not worship any god except me."' I replied, 'I will not
do it again.' There came a great man from the town of Pi-Boine to
give him a scroll bearing the destiny of the temple of Pi-Boine. This
said, 'Your will be with your word, promising to remain with him
[the god] throughout your days of life. Should calamity occur as
part of what is ordained, one man one fate.'

The second: I dreamt that I was in the necropolis of Memphis. A
foul death had seized a poor man; I lifted him upon myself and
brought him up to the Serapeum. I reached the processional way. A
ghost called out to me, 'Come to me; I have found a house which is
built.' I said to him, 'The house which is built is better than a house
which lacks its roof-beams.' He sat down in the middle of the way
and said to me, 'Bring your clover, the food for the 60,000 ibises.' I
said to him, 'It is in Pi-Thoth' ... He said to me, 'Bring it here
together with your things.' He added, 'You shall have a living soul
from the thirty-fifth day [halfway through the process of
mummification]. You shall die in Memphis, and you will be laid to
rest in the resting-place of the Serapeum. Hear the words which I
shall say to you. Go before Thoth and say, "Come to me my great
lord Thoth; beautiful is the lifetime long in festival." Go before Isis
and say, "Come to me my lady Isis; beautiful is burial within the
precincts of Memphis." Go before Osiris, and say before Osiris,
"Come to me my great lord Osiris; beautiful is this house upon the
deserts of Memphis, beautiful is the resting-place of the
Serapeum." All these things are written for you, all of them.'

At first sight these two dreams seem unconnected, but there are several common themes. There is the idea of assisting the weak: Hor receives help from his overseer, who turns out to be divine, and in the second dream he tries to extend help to the poor man. In both dreams there is insecurity. Powerful figures, the foreman and the ghost, interrogate the dreamer, and force him to admit his inadequacy. 'I will not do it again,' he says to the master, and the reply to the question about the clover is that he has left it at home. But above all it is clear that in both dreams he is being told the same thing, and it is a source of hope: to devote himself to the worship of Thoth, the god of learning, and to settle in Memphis. After this experience, Hor adopted the name Harthoth, or Horus-Thoth. We can only speculate on the state of mind which produced a conversion of this sort, but the one thing we cannot deny is that Hor believed that it happened. Awake, he had met Ptolemy VI; asleep, he saw Hermes Trismegistos. Was such a dream the sort of thing which could turn a man into a *katochos*?

In later life Hor of Sebennytos became involved in a scandal over the administration of the sacred ibises. He was disgraced, and may have lost his job. At one point, he wrote down a dream he had about his home town and the end of the world. Some of his ostraca are drafts for a somewhat self-righteous petition which he wrote to the king, to remind him of his success as a prophet of the gods and to obtain justice. As with Papyrus Rylands IX, we do not know the outcome. Like his four companions, Hor of Sebennytos goes into the darkness, and soon his sovereign followed him, thrown from a horse in Syria at a moment of what looked like triumph. One of the king's sons died at the age of twenty. The other wore the diadem after him, but not for very many lengthy days, since he was murdered by his uncle. One man, one fate. He of the quiet heart, as the Egyptians termed Osiris, knows every name.

'Such Is Osiris'

Hail to thee, Osiris son of [the sky-goddess] Nut, to whom was given the white crown of joy in the presence of the Ennead, whose awesomeness Atum created in the hearts of men, gods, spirits and the dead, who was given the sceptre in Heliopolis, great of transformations in Busiris ... of whom the great and powerful are in dread, for whom the great ones rise to their feet upon their mats ... Such is Osiris, sovereign of the gods, greatest power of heaven, ruler of the living, divine king [nesu] of those who are yonder ... When the gods see him, they give him praise; when the spirits see him, they embrace the ground. Thousands circulate around him in Abydos, and because of him those who are in the Underworld rejoice.

These words are taken from a funerary stela found at the site of Osiris' principal cult centre, Abydos in Upper Egypt. It is now in the Louvre, but many similar texts exist in other collections. Osiris was the god and ruler of the dead, and hymns in his honour are standard in the funerary cult throughout ancient Egyptian history. Although he features prominently in Egyptian religion, the origins of Osiris are a mystery. His name is written with three hieroglyphs, an open eye standing above a stylised seat, or throne, and the sign for a god. This combination does not make sense in terms of the conventional readings of these signs, and this suggests that the writing goes back to a remote time, when the values of the hieroglyphic script were still experimental. It may be that the name is foreign to Egyptian, but, if so, it has not been identified in any other language. The god is certainly ancient, but he is hardly mentioned in the earliest texts. Osiris begins to make a serious appearance in the Pyramid Texts, a body of hymns and incantations which are carved on the walls of the pyramids of the Fifth and Sixth Dynasties. Some of this material may have been centuries old before it was put into writing. In this early literature Osiris is mentioned sparingly, and only in contexts which make it clear that gods as well as men were held to be in awe of him. He is the dreaded lord of the afterlife, who demands respect even from the dead king whose monument the Pyramid Texts are intended to adorn. He is primeval, and he is best left to the silence.

Osiris is often thought to be an interloper at Abydos, the place which became the principal centre of his worship. In the earliest inscriptions from this site, there appears a deity known as Khenti-amentiu, 'the foremost of the westerners'. The westerners are the dead, who were thought to have joined the setting sun, and Osiris in later times fulfilled precisely the same role as Khenti-amentiu. This is too much of a coincidence, even for the complex overlap which characterises Egyptian religion. The likelihood is that Khenti-amentiu was a title of Osiris all along. The true name of the god was too awesome to be mentioned, and a less disturbing epithet was chosen to stand in its place.

The later appearances of Osiris are more attractive. In the First Intermediate Period, the time of Heqanakhte and his letters, any Egyptian who could afford a coffin or a funerary stela could be referred to as Osiris after his death. To go into the next life was to stand before Osiris for judgement, and to be vindicated against death and other enemies in the way that he had been. To be immortal was to become Osiris, and from this it followed that life with the god must be something to be desired. At some point,

Scene from the tomb of Nefertari in the Valley of the Queens. The goddesses Isis and Nephthys are shown on either side of the mummiform ram-headed figure surmounted by the disc of the setting sun. The hieroglyphic text identifies this figure as 'Re [the sun god], who sets as Osiris; Osiris, who rises as Re.'

perhaps in the Middle Kingdom, one of the earliest royal tombs at Abydos was rediscovered, and declared to be the burial place of the god himself. The phrase from the stela quoted above which mentions thousands of worshippers circulating around him probably refers to mass pilgrimages, similar in some ways to those held to this day around the sacred Ka'aba in Mecca. People went to Osiris in this life, as well as in the next.

Fragments of the fully developed myth of Osiris and his sister-wife Isis are found in numerous Egyptian sources, but the most detailed account is contained in Plutarch's *De Iside et Osiride*, which was composed in the years immediately before AD 120. In this version, the various strands which make up the mythology of Osiris have merged. Although a god, he had lived on earth as a king of Egypt, creating most of the benefits that were the essence of Egyptian civilisation. In this respect, he resembles the culture-heroes of other traditions. He was killed by the treachery of his brother, Seth, the god of disruption, but was brought back to life by the magic of Isis and his colleague Thoth, the ibis-headed god of wisdom. He is the dead king, wearing upon his head the white crown which was the symbol of the *nesu*, the divine aspect of the Pharaoh. His body was the land of Egypt, which was divided into provinces, each containing a relic of his limbs. He was also present in the waters of the Nile, which flooded and gave life each year to the earth of the Nile valley. But his true realm was not of this world, since he sat in perpetual rule over the dead. In this aspect, he is nothing less than the sun at night, giving light and sustenance to the netherworld. In several tombs of the New Kingdom, including that of Queen Nefertari, there is a scene featuring a staff or poll surmounted by the head of a ram coloured green like the vegetation of Egypt. The hieroglyphic caption to this scene reads, 'This is [the sun god] Re who sets as Osiris; this is Osiris who rises as Re.' Rich or poor, literate or illiterate, the ancient Egyptians were the heirs of this god who had once ruled their land, and before whose judgement they would eventually find themselves. Some of the twelve characters in this book will have died with his name on their lips, or in their ears, and it is no coincidence that he recurs throughout these pages. One of his other names was Onnofri, 'the perfect (or complete) being', and as such he can be seen as the personification of ancient Egypt.

Notes to the Text

1   *Egyptian Antiquities in the Nile Valley* (Methuen, 1932), p. 435,
    with the king's name spelt Ramses. Amun and Re are here
    the names of military regiments.
2   This, and some later commentaries, are listed in the
    suggestions for further reading at the end of the book.
    Extracts given in translation are cited as UPZ followed by the
    text number.
3   *Urkunden der Ptolemäerzeit* (=UPZ) 9.
4   UPZ 3.
5   UPZ 6.
6   UPZ 63.
7   UPZ 12.
8   UPZ 77.
9   Demotic Papyrus Bologna 3173.
10 Ostracon Hermitage 1129.
11 UPZ 78.
12 Hor Text 8.

Picture Credits

Chapter 1

Base of Statue of King Djoser, found by the Step Pyramid complex at
Saqqara (Service des Antiquités d'Egypte)

The Step Pyramid at Saqqara. (*Sakkarah: The Monuments of Zoser* (1939)
Etienne Drioton et Jean-Philippe Lauer, Le Caire, Imprimerie de
l'Institut français d'archéologie orientale, plate 14)

Chapter 2

Heqanakhte Letter (Metropolitan Museum of Art, New York, Rogers
Fund and Edward S. Harkness Gift, 1922 [22.3.516])

The god Amun receiving offerings from Pharaoh Seti I (photo: AKG
London/François Guénet)

Painting of an agricultural scene, from tomb of Ity at Gebelein
(Werner Forman Archive / Egyptian Museum, Turin)

Chapter 3

Detail of relief showing Queen Hatshepsut (Hirmer Archiv)

Hatshepsut's temple at Deir el-Bahri (Hirmer Archiv)

Queen Hatshepsut as a kneeling Pharaoh, found in a relief in Karnak
temple (AKG Berlin/Werner Forman)

Chapter 4

Royal family making offerings to Aten – detail from a relief found at
Amarna (Cairo Egyptian Museum; photo:AKG London/Erich
Lessing)

Statue of Horemheb as a scribe (Metropolitan Museum of Art , New
York, Gift of Mr and Mrs V. Everit Macy, 1923 [23.10.1])
Statue of the goddess Mut (Hirmer Archiv)

Chapter 5
Detail of painting from Queen Nefertari's tomb (Werner Forman
Archive/E. Strouhal)
Portrait of Prince Khaemwiese, from relief found at Saqqara,
(Louvre, Paris)
The avenue leading to Prince Khaemwiese's Serapeum. Drawing by
Barbot. (The Archive of Hor (1976) J. D. Ray, Egypt Exploration
Society, frontispiece)

Chapter 6
Headless statue of King Darius, Susa, Iran (Cambridge Ancient History,
plates to vol. 4 (1995), John Boardman (ed.), figure 22b)
Demotic Papyrus petition (John Rylands Library, Manchester)

Chapter 7
Statue of Nectanebo (Metropolitan Museum of Modern Art, New
York, Rogers Fund, 1934 [34.2.1])
Detail of the Metternich Stela (Metropolitan Museum of Art , New
York, Fletcher Fund, 1950 [50.85])
Sketch by Apollonios (Rijksmuseum, Leiden)

Chapter 8
Stela of a dream interpreter (Cairo Egyptian Museum [CG27567])
A painted shroud, from Memphis (Egyptian Museum, Berlin; photo:
AKG London/Erich Lessing)

Epilogue
Scene from the tomb of Nefertari, in the Valley of the Queens (AKG
Berlin/Werner Forman)

Suggestions for Further Reading

THERE ARE as many general books on ancient Egypt and Egyptology as there are angels dancing on the head of a pin, and any short list is invidious. However, a start can be made with John Baines and Jaromir Malek, *Atlas of Ancient Egypt* (Phaidon, 1980); Barry J. Kemp, *Ancient Egypt. Anatomy of a Civilization* (Routledge, 1989); Jaromir Malek (ed.), *Cradles of Civilization: Egypt* (Weldon Russell, 1993); Ian Shaw and Paul Nicholson, *The British Museum Dictionary of Ancient Egypt* (British Museum Press, 1995); Stephen Quirke, *Ancient Egyptian Religion* (British Museum Press, 1992, rep. 1997); Charles Freeman, *The Legacy of Ancient Egypt* (Andromeda, 1997); Vivian Davies and Renée Friedman, *Egypt* (British Museum Press, 1998); and *The Oxford Illustrated History of Ancient Egypt* (ed. Ian Shaw, Oxford, 2000).

Imhotep

The best general book on the Step Pyramid area is Jean-Philippe Lauer's *Saqqara. The Royal Cemetery of Memphis. Excavations and Discoveries since 1850* (Thames & Hudson, 1976). There is also much in Mark Lehner's *The Complete Pyramids* (Thames & Hudson, 1997). An account of the worship of Imhotep can be found in Dietrich Wildung's *Egyptian Saints. Deification in Pharaonic Egypt* (New York,

1977). The Late-Period cults at Saqqara, and the Egypt Exploration Society's excavations at the site, are described by H. S. Smith, *A Visit to Ancient Egypt* (Warminster, 1974). There is also a short treatment by J. D. Ray, 'The World of North Saqqâra', in *World Archaeology* 10/2 (October 1978), pp. 149–57.

Heqanakhte

The indispensable edition of Heqanakhte's letters is T. G. H. James, *The Hekanakhte Papers and other Early Middle Kingdom Documents* (Metropolitan Museum of Art, New York, 1962). There is also a convenient treatment of two of the letters in R. B. Parkinson, *Voices from Ancient Egypt. An Anthology of Middle Kingdom Writings* (British Museum Press, 1991). The translations given in this chapter are my own, like the others in this book, but I am aware that I cannot improve on Parkinson's. The archaeology of Thebes (Luxor) in this period was dealt with in H. E. Winlock's *The Rise and Fall of the Middle Kingdom in Thebes* (New York, 1947), while more up-to-date information can be found in G. Vörös, *Temple on the Pyramid of Thebes* (Budapest, 1998). The Wisdom of Ankhsheshonq is translated in Miriam Lichtheim, *Ancient Egyptian Literature III. The Late Period* (California, 1980). Agatha Christie's *Death Comes as the End* was first published in 1945.

Hatshepsut

Some of this chapter explores themes briefly sketched in a study by the present author which appeared in *History Today* 44/5 (May 1994), pp. 23–9. A useful general account is Joyce Tyldesley's *Hatchepsut. The Female Pharaoh* (Viking, 1996), and there is also the volume by Susanne Ratié, *La reine Hatchepsout. Sources et problèmes*

(Leiden, 1979). Women in ancient Egypt in general are the subject of Gay Robins, *Women in Ancient Egypt* (British Museum Press, 1993) and Joyce Tyldesley, *Daughters of Isis* (Penguin, 1994). There is also much in Peter F. Dorman's *The Monuments of Senenmut* (Kegan Paul International, 1988). The pictorial graffiti are discussed by Edward F. Wente in *Journal of Near Eastern Studies* 43 (1984), pp. 47–54. The story of the Shipwrecked Sailor can be found in R. B. Parkinson, *The Tale of Sinuhe and Other Ancient Egyptian Poems 1940–1640 BC* (Oxford, 1997), and the obelisk inscriptions are in Miriam Lichtheim, *Ancient Egyptian Literature II. The New Kingdom* (California, 1976).

Horemheb

The literature on the Amarna period is considerable, but the role of Horemheb tends not to be emphasised. He can be found, almost as a postscript, in the standard histories of ancient Egypt and the Eighteenth Dynasty. The Memphite tomb of Horemheb is described in Geoffrey T. Martin, *The Hidden Tombs of Memphis. New Discoveries from the Time of Tutankhamun and Ramesses the Great* (Thames & Hudson, 1991). The inscriptions of Horemheb, both as regent and king, can be found in William J. Murnane, *Texts from the Amarna Period in Egypt* (Scholars Press, Atlanta, 1995).

Khaemwise

There is a short treatment of this prince in Joyce Tyldesley's *Ramesses. Egypt's Greatest Pharaoh* (Viking, 2000). The tomb-complex known as KV5 is the subject of Kent Weeks's *The Lost Tomb* (Weidenfeld & Nicolson, 1998). The activity of Khaemwise at Memphis is discussed in an article by J. Malek in *Studies in*

Pharaonic Religion and Society in Honour of J. Gwyn Griffiths (ed. A. B. Lloyd, Egypt Exploration Society, 1992). The fragmentary accounts of Khaemwise's ship can be studied in J. J. Janssen, Two Ancient Egyptian Ship's Logs (Leiden, 1961). Two of the demotic Setne-stories can be found translated in Miriam Lichtheim, Ancient Egyptian Literature III.

The Petition of Petiese

This remarkable text has been little advertised, but there is a useful paraphrase in the opening chapter of Serge Sauneron, The Priests of Ancient Egypt (Evergreen Books, 1960). The pioneering translation is by F. Ll. Griffith (Demotic Papyri in the John Rylands Library, Manchester, 1909), though this is to be found only in specialised libraries. There is also a study in German by G. Vittman (Wiesbaden, 1998). The cosmopolitan aspect of the period can be found in J. M. Cook, The Persian Empire (Dent, 1983), The Cambridge Ancient History (second edn), Volume IV (Cambridge, 1988), and Amélie Kuhrt, The Ancient Near East c. 3000–330 BC, Volume II (Routledge, 1995). A treatment of the various ancient canals across the isthmus of Suez can be found in James K. Hoffmeier, Israel in Egypt (Oxford, 1996).

Nectanebo

As with Hatshepsut, some of the chapter on Nectanebo is developed from an article which appeared in History Today 42/2 (February 1992), pp. 38–44. There is a good general account of the period by Alan B. Lloyd in Cambridge Ancient History (second edn), Volume VI: The Fourth Century BC (Cambridge, 1994). A more traditional dates-and-battles account can be found in P. G. Elgood, The

Later Dynasties of Egypt (Oxford, 1951). The international background is well illustrated in Paul Cartledge's *Agesilaos and the Crisis of Sparta* (Duckworth, 1987). The role of Nectanebo in later legend can be studied in George Cary, *The Mediaeval Alexander* (Cambridge, 1956, repr. 1967) and Richard Stoneman, *The Greek Alexander Romance* (Penguin, 1991).

Hor of Sebennytos and His Companions

There is no complete account of the characters from the Serapeum in any language, but the indispensable introduction is the treatment by Dorothy Thompson in *Memphis under the Ptolemies* (Princeton, 1988). There is good comparative material in Jane Rowlandson (ed.), *Women and Society in Greek and Roman Egypt. A Sourcebook* (Cambridge, 1998). The Greek papyri were published by Ulrich Wilcken, in his magisterial *Urkunden der Ptolemäerzeit* (Berlin and Leipzig, 1927), while a preliminary study of the Hor ostraca can be found in J. D. Ray, *The Archive of Hor* (Egypt Exploration Society, 1976). N. J. Reich's study of Apollonios appeared in *Mizraim* I (1933), pp. 147–77. These are specialist publications, but there is a useful account of the Hor discoveries in Vivian Davies and Renée Friedman's *Egypt*. An excellent idea of what Graeco-Roman Egyptians looked like can be found in the illustrated catalogue *Ancient Faces* (ed. Susan Walker, British Museum Press, 2000).

Acknowledgement

SOME OF the material on Hatshepsut (Chapter 3) and Nectanebo II (Chapter 7) first appeared in articles for *History Today*. I am grateful to its Editor for being able to reuse it in a different form here.

Index